THE BIRD TABLE BOOK

THE
BIRD TABLE BOOK

Tony Soper

Illustrations by Robert Gillmor

DAVID & CHARLES
Newton Abbot   London   North Pomfret (Vt)

For Tim

By the same author
Beside the Sea (with Hilary Soper)
Birdwatch
Discovering Animals
Discovering Birds
Everyday Birds
The National Trust Book of the Coast
Owls (with John Sparks)
A Passion for Birds
Penguins (with John Sparks)
The Shell Book of Beachcombing
Wildlife Begins at Home
The Wreck of the Torrey Canyon (with
Crispin Gill and Frank Booker)

British Library Cataloguing in Publication Data

Soper, Tony
    The bird table book. – 5th ed., rev.
    1. Birds – Great Britain   2. Garden fauna
    – Great Britain
    I. Title
    639.9′782941   QL690.G7

    ISBN 0–7153–8866–5

© Topy Soper 1965, 1966, 1973, 1977, 1986

First published October 1965
Revised editions 1966, 1973, 1977
Fifth edition 1986
Reprinted 1987 (twice)
Reprinted 1988
Reprinted 1989

Phototypeset by Typesetters (Birmingham) Ltd,
Smethwick, West Midlands
and printed in Great Britain
by Redwood Burn Ltd, Trowbridge
for David & Charles Publishers plc
Brunel House   Newton Abbot   Devon

Published in the United States of America
by David & Charles Inc
North Pomfret   Vermont 05053   USA

Contents

Jay

Waxwing

Green
Woodpecker

Hoopoe

Rose-ringed
Parakeet

RG

Preface

Many crumbs have been eaten by many robins since this book was first launched twenty-one years ago. And interest in bird gardening continues to grow, as my postman will confirm! So this new edition reflects the changing character of the bird table scene. When the first *Bird Table Book* was written, no siskin had ever taken a peanut, so far as we know. Now they are two-a-penny on mesh baskets, joining reed buntings and lesser spotted woodpeckers, and also ring-necked parakeets and other exotic creatures.

It is clear that more species are learning to take advantage of bird tables and feeding stations. Just as well, when so much of their natural feeding ground is being swallowed up for unsympathetic development. All the more reason to try to create a house and garden which takes into account the requirements of wildlife as well as your own.

Feeding birds (and hedgehogs, badgers and toads, too) is a rewarding activity. Not only are these creatures good to see about the house, but their relationships with each other, with man, and with their surroundings, are of absorbing interest. So spare them an honest crust, with a bit of cheese as well.

(*opposite*) Any of these colourful birds might visit your garden, some as residents, others as winter or summer visitors

1 The bird garden

Although the idea of living in a cave may seem to have its attractions, most of us inhabit a house. And in building ourselves a nest we inevitably disturb and deprive the previous 'owners', so it is good to feel that there are ways in which we may redress the balance. Gardens, and to a certain extent houses, provide the basic requirements of food and shelter for a whole community of wild plants and animals. As time goes by, more and more species are learning to visit garden feeding stations and take advantage of man's activities and generosity. In Devon, for instance, forty different species have taken food from a rural garden. Reed buntings, siskins and great spotted woodpeckers are examples of birds which are increasingly welcomed in suburban gardens in many parts of the British Isles. Exotic birds like the hoopoe, visiting southern England in the summer when they overshoot the channel, are as often as not seen in private gardens, enjoying the insect harvest of a well-kept lawn.

But while rarities are of interest, far and away the greatest pleasure of bird gardening is the year-in, year-out companion-ship of a group of individuals which have thrown in their lot with you and become residents. The swallows and house-

Robins are happy to share your garden with you, especially if you provide them with a home; a quart kettle makes a good nestbox, but fix it firmly in a sheltered position and make sure the spout points downwards to act as a drainpipe (*John Clements*)

House Sparrow

Wren

Dunnock

Chaffinch

Robin

Birds' bills give a clue to their diet. Finches have nutcracker bills adapted for cracking and crushing; birds with slimmer, more pointed, bills tend to search for caterpillars and insects

martins of summer are a joy to welcome, but the robin which feeds from the hand and sings through the winter brings a deeper sense of community with his belonging.

An open well-kept lawn is almost essential to a bird garden. It gives a clear view and makes a happy hunting area for birds searching for ants, cockchafer grubs and worms. Worms are much misunderstood creatures and it is certainly a mistake to try to kill them off. They are useful; they aereate, drain and fertilise the soil, and though wormcasts may be unsightly they consist of fine rich soil. Spread them with a lawn rake or drag a weighted piece of wire netting over them before mowing. In autumn, don't be too quick to sweep up fallen leaves; worms like them (especially willow and cherry), and birds like worms.

The bird garden should have a varied terrain, with changes of level, corners, miniature cliffs, valleys, hills, ravines, and low dry-stone walls – all features which will provide a diversity of insect life and rich foraging areas. Flower beds and neat borders do not offer much of interest, and an over-tidy garden is an unexciting hunting-ground. Try to organise a rock bank or low wall in a warm or south-facing part of the garden, so that it is less likely to be snowed up in winter. A reasonable amount of 'jungle', plenty of berry-bearing trees and shrubs, and a good lawn, are the things to aim for.

11

If you've room for a patch of rough grass and nettles, please write them into your plan. A nettle-bed is highly productive of insects and will provide sustenance for many small birds. Cultivate the attitude of mind which sees a nettle-bed not as weeds but as a butterfly garden! Butterflies like their nettles to be in full sunlight. Trim the plants in rotation every few weeks to keep a ready supply of fresh juicy shoots.

Incidentally, if you are having a new house built, be very careful that the builders set the topsoil aside for subsequent replacement before they start crashing about with bulldozers. Builders are all too ready to bury your vital topsoil under tons of useless subsoil, and you will find it is a long uphill grind to produce a fertile garden.

The best bird-garden boundary ever devised is the Devon hedgerow. A wide foundation-bank with rough stone and greenery, with ivy and ferns and wild flowers growing out of it, and topped with a close hawthorn or hazel hedge, is a bird paradise. One of the many beauties of a hedgerow is that it provides a variety of food in winter time when natural resources are at their lowest. Thrushes will eat berry-pulp and pass the pips. Then the finches and tits will eat the pips as they forage along the hedgerow bottom. Dead leaves and debris shelter hibernating flies and insects, spiders, woodlice and centipedes, all of which are good for wrens, tits and dunnocks. In the hedge itself, the leaves stay attached and provide warmth and cover through the winter. The bank harbours yet more grubs and insects, wintering aphids and their eggs, chrysalids, and so on. Common hedgerow birds are blackbird, thrush, chaffinch, yellowhammer, dunnock, robin, wren, whitethroat, linnet, great tit, blue tit, long-tailed tit, and willow warbler. So one of the most distressing country sights is the bulldozing of hedgerows in order to make bigger fields.

If you haven't the space to develop a Devon hedgerow, then a thorn, holly or hazel hedge will do very well instead. Put a couple of crab apple trees in it: they will provide useful stand-by food supplies in hard weather. Fieldfares will hack open the apples, and chaffinches will eat the pips.

Generally speaking, it is as well to avoid planting coarse thick-leaved evergreens. The rhododendrons and laurels beloved of town councils are unpromising bird habitats, taking light from the ground and not offering many insects in return. If you have lots of room then you might plant an isolated group of pine or larch in the hope of attracting goldcrests and crossbills. But have *some* evergreens, because they provide autumn and winter cover for roosting birds. A berry-bearing holly will serve a double purpose. Have one tall tree at least, a poplar for instance, and your thrush will sing from the top-most branch.

If you are lucky enough to have some old fruit trees, keep one or two for the birds. Leave the fruit on them and it will be welcomed by thrushes, fieldfares and redwings in the winter. Tits are also worth encouraging in orchards because they control the bug population. If you make sure there is a plentiful water supply, they may eat less of your fruit.

And when your trees die of old age, leave them to rot gently in peace, because in decay they are an important part of the woodland cycle. They provide food and shelter for yet more variety of species and, in principle, the greater the diversity of habitat you are able to offer, the healthier your garden will be. Those who scoff at gardens with nettle-beds and fungus-covered rotting tree trunks are simply displaying their ignorance of what life is all about! But if you want to 'improve' your rotting tree trunk, grow a climbing plant such as clematis to cover it.

In planting new trees, pick native rather than foreign species. Not only are they better adapted to the climate, but they are better integrated with the pattern of our flora and fauna. A mature oak or lime supports so much life that it is a complete community in itself, but of course it needs a great deal of space and time to reach maturity, so you may choose to plant quick-growing species like ash, elm, birch or willow. Remember that trees do not all have the same soil require-ments. The easiest method of finding out what does well is to look around your neighbourhood, but a nurseryman will help. And remember that birds prefer red fruits above all!

Berry-bearing trees and shrubs
YEW. *Taxus baccata.* Evergreen. As a tree it may grow exceptionally to 90ft (27m), but can be clipped.

As a bush of only 6ft (1.8m) or so it makes a good hedge and provides nesting sites. Slow growing, it may be fifteen years before it fruits and it may live for 2,000 years. A very

Peanuts are a favourite food, but don't provide them during the breeding season when they might be taken back to nestlings by inexperienced parents (*Jonathan Player/Ardea, London*)

good bird tree, the fleshy red berries are favourites with thrushes and starlings. The birds eat the pulp, but pass the poisonous seed without harm. Yew foliage and bark are also poisonous.

HAZEL. *Corylus avellana*. Deciduous bush, best on chalky soil, branching from the ground and growing to 15ft (4.5m). Prefers rich soil, not too wet. Useful as hedgerow plant although it doesn't provide good nest sites (good pea sticks though). Nut harvest in August/September.

BARBARY (Common barbary). *Berberis vulgaris*. Deciduous. Grows thickly branched to 5 or 6ft (1.5 or 1.8m). The coral-red berries have a high vitamin C content and are eaten by most birds, particularly blackbirds. Cultivated species and varieties: *B. darwinii*, evergreen, is the commonest form, growing to about 10ft (3m); purple fruit; can be planted as hedge. *B. aggregata* 'Buccaneer', deciduous, has long-lasting berries and grows to 9ft (2.7m). *B. wilsonae*, deciduous, translucent coral berries; formidable thorns make it a good hedge plant. All the barbarys are easy to grow and provide thick cover and weed-free ground underneath.

COTONEASTER. *Cotoneaster integerrima*. Useful because it fruits late, after hawthorn and before the ivy harvest. Thrushes, blackbirds, finches and tits like its rich red berries. Grows almost anywhere. Cultivated forms come in a wide variety, from a few inches to 25ft (7.5m) in height. *C. dammeri* and *C. prostrata* are trailers, small but ever-spreading; *C. buxifolia*, *C. francheti* and *C. lactea* are evergreen wall-climbers, growing to 5, 10 and 15ft (1.5, 3 and 4.5m) respectively; *C. horizontalis* and *C. rotundifolia* are deciduous and grow to about 4ft (1.2m), with fan-like

Birds must bathe in order to keep their plumage in condition (*John Markham, Bruce Coleman Ltd*)

branches. *C. simonsii* makes an effective hedge, and produces good berries.

HAWTHORN (or Whitethorn). *Crategus monogyna*. Makes excellent boy-proof hedge and grows quickly almost anywhere. Blackbirds, fieldfares, and redwings all love the scarlet haws. Spiky branches offer good cover for nests. Can be cut to shape but is best if allowed to fruit and flower. Good for insects. Do not confuse this tree with the blackthorn, whose sloes are not much liked by birds.

ROWAN (Mountain Ash). *Sorbus aucuparia*. A top-class bird tree, not too fussy about soil but it needs light. Grows 15 to 25ft (4.5 to 7.5m) and spreads. Mistle thrushes are very fond of the bunches of brilliant coral-red fruit. Fruits in August. Every Highland croft used to be surrounded by rowans, because the tree was supposed to have magic powers and guard against evil. *Sorbus vilmorinii* is a Chinese species which bears big berries and only grows to 12ft (3.6m).

HOLLY. *Ilex aquifolium*. Makes an excellent evergreen and catproof hedge. Thrushes and starlings like the berries, but these only come freely from an unclipped plant. Hollies are either male or female, and only the female produces berries. They also tend to be difficult to grow, so it may be best to buy from a nurseryman when you can be sure of getting a strong female. There must be one male somewhere near, of course, for cross-fertilisation. Otherwise, plant several and hope for the best. The cultivated forms are the more reliable. 'Golden King' is a small holly reaching to 10ft (3m) and bearing a good berry crop. 'Madame Briot' grows to 18ft (5.4m) and bears golden berries. Prefers well-drained soil.

SPINDLE. *Euonymus europaeus*. A bushy and ornamental shrub, growing to 15ft (4.5m). Prefers chalk or lime-rich soil. Pink and orange fruit and beautiful autumn colours.

LIME (Linden). *Tilia cordata*. A large tree, growing exceptionally to 150ft (45m), but very amenable to pruning. One of the few forest trees to be pollinated by insects. There is a species of aphid which prefers lime trees, and exudes a sticky honeydew which attracts insects, especially bees, so that limes are humming with insect sounds and movement in summer. Birds come for the insects in summer, and for the fruits in autumn.

IVY. *Hedera helix*. Good birdman's plant, which thrives in poor soil. Climbs or carpets the ground, but only flowers when it reaches light. Very attractive to insects when it flowers in September/October. One of latest plants to flower, berries sustain birds in late winter. Wrens roost in it. Much maligned as a tree-strangler, but in fact it does no harm until it reaches the rare stage of totally covering the crown. Encourage it.

ELDER. *Sambucus nigra.* Some gardeners think of elder as a weed, but the bird gardener grows it because tits and thrushes like the purple berries and the early leaves make good nesting cover. Fast grower and takes plenty of pruning punishment. Hardy. Grows almost anywhere. Over 32 bird species visited it in an RSPB survey. Avoid cultivated versions.

GUELDER ROSE. *Viburnum opulus.* Grows to 18ft (5.4m), produces large, flat clusters of flowers and red berries. The cultivated variety, *V. compactum*, is useful for a small garden, as it can be kept to 6ft (1.8m). The species of Guelder Rose often sold as the Snowball bush is sterile and useless for birds.

HONEYSUCKLE. *Lonicera periclymenum.* A liana which entwines and climbs trees or bushes, or any man-made framework, but is very strong and will distort a growing plant with its vigorous coils. The nectar is difficult to reach and only insects with long probosci, such as the privet hawk-moth, can get at it. Blackbirds, tits and warblers like the berries of the wild or cultivated forms.

FIRETHORN. *Pyracantha coccinea.* In the top ten of berry-producers, very much appreciated by thrushes. *P. atlantoides* offers good cover for nests.

There are, of course, plenty of other trees and bushes which produce bird berries and you may care to experiment. Fruit trees of all kinds are highly suitable, and your conscience may even allow you to take a certain amount for your own table.

CRAB APPLE. The native wild version is *Malus pumila*, but the ornamental variety 'Golden Hornet' is recommended, as well as the Siberian crab apple *Malus robusta*. Their fruits are taken by thrushes, even waxwings, but only after frosts have softened them, so they offer sustenance very late in the winter, even into February, when natural bird food is short.

Sunflowers, if left to seed, are irresistible to tits, nuthatches and finches, and may even entice goldcrests if you are lucky. Forget-me-nots and cornflowers also produce seeds which are attractive to finches. (At nesting time, goldfinches may gather bunches of forget-me-not flowers and use them as building materials.) Other useful birdseed plants are cosmos, china asters, scabious, evening primrose, antirrhinum and common field-poppy.

Garden plants which attract butterflies
Spring: thrift, honesty, sweet rocket, valerian.
Summer: bugle, sweet william, lavender, catmint, phlox, hyssop, buddleia.
Autumn: heliotrope, golden rod, aster, michaelmas daisy, iceplant (but not cultivars such as 'Autumn Joy').

Plant in masses if possible and in full sunlight. Buddleia is a first class plant for attracting butterflies which provide caterpillars much appreciated by birds, but avoid the pale mauve and white versions and the deep-coloured cultivars. 'Royal Red' has dark flowers which do the trick. If you have several bushes cut one back around April to delay its flowering and lengthen the season.

Weeds
Many weeds produce seeds which are sought after by birds. Finches, especially goldfinches, are keen on thistle (ornamental varieties are less likely to run riot, yet produce acceptable seeds). Knapweed, teazle, ragwort and nettles are all attractive to birds, if not the human gardener. Grow them in a sunny, sheltered corner.

2   Water

It is absolutely vital to provide a constant supply of clean water for your birds. Some can last a long time without drinking, some will die within a few days, but none can manage entirely without water for it is essential to the proper functioning of their bodies. Although birds do not sweat, they lose water, mainly by excretion, and must make up the loss. They will derive some water from their food, and the rest from drinking. Tree-living species may sip from foliage after rain, but most birds will visit ponds and streams. Some will fill their bills, then raise their heads to let the water run down their throats; some will keep their bills in the water; some will sip from the surface of the water as they fly past. Swifts and swallows even bathe in flight, dipping under with a quick splash as they go by. Swifts simply bathe in rain while in flight.

Birds also need water to help with the continuing problem of keeping their plumage in order. Quite apart from the fact that feathers are a vital part of their flying apparatus, plumage acts as an insulator and regulates body temperature. To be fully efficient, the feathers must be kept in good condition, and feather maintenance looms large in a bird's life. Bathing is the first move in a ccomplicated series of events.

The object of the bath is to wet the plumage without actually soaking it (if the feathers become too wet they may deteriorate). Birds will sometimes bathe in drizzle, but if they are caught out in a heavy downpour they will hunch into a special position, reaching upwards and tightening their feathers so that the rain pours off quickly.

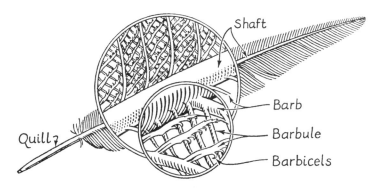

After the bath the bird will shake itself and begin 'oiling'. With the tail twisted to one side, it will reach down with its bill to collect fatty oil from its preen gland. Then, very carefully, it will rub the oil into the feathers, all over the body. The difficult stage is when it wants to oil its head. To do this, it will use a foot, first oiling the foot and then scratching the grease onto the head. Next comes the preening session, when the bird will nibble and stroke all its feathers. This may take a long time, and afterwards the bird will stretch and settle itself until its plumage is in full flying and insulating order – all systems go.

The supreme engineering triumph of the bird is its feathers: purpose-built extensions of the skin, horny growths similar in origin to our own fingernails. Light but strong, amongst other things they provide lift surfaces which, powered by all that muscle, give the bird flight capability. Their surface area is large, compared with the weight involved, and their ingenious design allows for continuous maintenance and ruffle-smoothing. And when a part has come to the end of its useful life,

Sketches of a young blackbird, preening after bathing

after much wear and tear, it may be replaced without withdrawing the aircraft from service.

The power of flight gives birds the key to world travel. A tern may spend the summer nesting in the Arctic, then strike south to 'winter' in the Antarctic, incredible though that may seem to us. From its point of view it is simply making the best of both worlds. Not all birds use those feathers to propel them across the world. Flight has other values. Instant escape from enemies, airborne invasion of an area rich in caterpillars, or fast approach and capture of prey: all these things are possible with feathers. And different birds have different designs to fit them best for different purposes. A swift has narrow, swept-back wings, designed for speed and aerial fly-chasing; its take-off and landing performance is poor. A pheasant has broad, short wings, giving a powerful near-vertical take-off for instant escape, although it pays for the facility by having a low endurance, needing to land again within a short distance – far enough away, though, to keep out of trouble.

Even for flightless birds, which might at first seem to make nonsense of all those years of research and development, the wings are important pieces of equipment. A penguin's flipper may seem an un-feather-like, hard, rigid structure, but it is in fact a modified wing superbly built for flying – *underwater*; the bird is a master submariner.

Wings are not only used for flying. They may be used as legs, as when a swallow struggles to take a few shaky steps on the ground. On occasion they may be used as advertisement hoardings, their colour-reflecting surfaces being held up and displayed in order to intimidate a rival or impress a partner. The wings are then playing their part in the process of avian communication.

Feathers, too, have functions beyond providing lift and flight. Soft down feathers insulate the body and keep it warm; waterproof outer contour feathers repel rain and keep it dry. In some species feathers may help to guide flying insects into the gaping maw and in others feathers may protect the face from the stings of bees and wasps. So feather maintenance is a vital part of a bird's daily life. Much time is devoted to bathing, oiling and preening, keeping the tools of the trade in trim and keeping the bird dry, warm and ready for instant take-off. If they are badly damaged, they are replaced as part of normal growth. In the ordinary course of wear and tear they will be replaced as part of a continuous moult: a staggered process because at any given time the bird must not be at a disadvantage with too many feathers out of action. However, ducks and geese do in fact follow a somewhat different plan, moulting all their flight feathers in one fell swoop, lying doggo and flightless for a few weeks after the breeding season while they grow a new suit for the migration flight. At this period they present a sorry appearance, but even this 'eclipse' plumage serves a purpose, camouflaging the birds at the time when they are most vulnerable.

A partial albino male Blackbird

White, or partially white, birds often appear in gardens. A survey which analysed over three thousand occurrences of this albinism showed that the six species most commonly affected were blackbird, sparrow, starling, swallow, rook and jackdaw. Except in the case of the swallow, the phenomenon affects birds which tend to lead somewhat sedentary and sociable lives. The causes are not easily defined: they may have something to do with a dietary deficiency, perhaps associated with a high intake of 'artificial' food offered at bird tables. Certainly albinism appears to be most often noticed in urban and suburban habitats, where bird table food provides a significant proportion of a blackbird's diet.

Whatever the reason, it is a fact that the blackbird is more prone to albinism, partial or total, than any other species. In the true albino, pigment is completely absent, even the beak, legs and eyes being colourless, but most often the condition is partial, with the plumage revealing a patch of white, or perhaps just one white feather. The extent of the whiteness may vary from season to season, and albino or part-albino young may be produced by normal parents as easily as normal young may be produced by albino parents. An individual may show more white as the years go by. Any feather on the bird may be affected, but the head is particularly prone. One can't help wondering to what extent the white blackbird is at a disadvantage, because at the least it becomes conspicuous and therefore extra vulnerable to predation. But the suburban habitat, while it may be partly responsible for the problem, is at least a relatively protected environment. So perhaps it is a case of six of one and half-a-dozen of the other.

Whiteness is not the only genetic abnormality suffered by blackbirds. Other 'isms' produce varying intensities of reddishness and yellowishness (erythrism and xanthochroism). In our own garden as I write this we have a gloriously honey-coloured blackbird, an example of leucism, where the normal pigment is diluted and paled. Another common plumage abnormality is melanism, where the bird has too much of the dark pigment eumelanin. These melanistic forms have an exaggerated blackness. Pheasants provide the most commonly seen examples of this.

Whatever the colour of our blackbird's plumage, its maintenance is of great importance. At the bird bath he shows his feathers off to great advantage: the wings outspread, the

Blackbird - oiling

handsome tail held down at a right angle and fanned out to show its full spread. Even in the depths of winter birds must bathe their plumage frequently as part of the process of keeping their insulating and flying suit in full working order. Bedraggled feathers waste body heat and make for inefficient flying, and in winter lost energy is not easily replaced.

Unless you are lucky enough to have a stream or pond in your garden you will obviously have to provide water in some form or another. The bird bath is the obvious answer, although it is not the best. However, if you are short of space, it will suffice. The simplest version is an upturned dustbin lid, supported by three bricks or sunk into the ground, although if you sink it, it will be more difficult to keep ice-free in winter.

An advantage of keeping it off the ground is that you are providing extra foraging ground and possibly a toad-hole underneath! The water depth should vary from about 1in (2.5cm) deep to not more than 4in (10cm), and there should be a shallow approach as most birds prefer shallow water for bathing. Always use clean water and keep the bath up to its marks.

If you jib at introducing dustbin lids into your garden, use any similarly-shaped, shallow bowl, but beware of the ornamental, plastic, so-called 'bird baths' which garden shops sell and which may have a slippery slope leading to a cavernous well. Whatever kind of bowl you use, put it in shade and within reasonable range of cover and safety, but not so close that a cat may lurk and pounce. A point to remember is that birds get rather excited and preoccupied about their bathing; they tend, therefore, to be more vulnerable then than at other times.

At all times it is important to avoid letting the bath go dry, and it is especially important to keep it ice-free in winter. If the bowl is breakable, put a chunk of softwood into it so that if the water freezes the strain will be taken by the wood and not the bowl. I have seen a blue tit cracking a thin layer of ice, but this only served to show how badly it needed water. If your bath is a few inches off the ground, you can put one of those slow-burning nightlights underneath but, best of all, put an aquarium immersion heater in the pool, covered with some gravel. Connected to a thermostat (also submerged), it will control the water temperature so that there is a permanently ice-free area. Provided the mains lead is of a suitable outdoor type and the connections are properly made, no danger is involved. Both the immersion heater and the thermostat can be obtained from any aquarium dealer (or from Queensborough Fisheries, see page 32). These gadgets are very reliable, but if you want to be extra cautious get an electrician to wire *two* of the heaters in parallel. Then if one fails the other will still carry on.

Do *not* use salt, glycerine, or anti-freeze of any kind to keep the water ice-free. These chemicals will cause havoc to a bird's feathers at a time when they should be in first-class condition to keep out the cold. People sometimes ask why birds bathe so much in freezing weather, and the answer must now be obvious. To keep warm, the feathers must be efficient, and to have efficient feathers the bird must go through the preening ritual which starts with a bath.

While a bird bath will serve its purpose quite adequately, a properly-stocked and regulated pool with oxygenating plants and fish is infinitely preferable, and much more rewarding. The water should be very shallow, but if you are going to make a special pond you may want to have a deeper section in which to raise fish in the hope of attracting kingfishers and herons. Design the pond so that there is a gently-shelving shallow area leading to the main depth of 18in (46cm) or so. And provide a gently-sloping approach to the shallow area so that hedgehogs and grass snakes, and other welcome animals, can come to drink and bathe (and get out again!).

Constructing your own garden pond
Garden ponds give a full measure of pleasure to the owner. It has to be said, however, that there is a certain amount of hard

labour involved in the making of them. Some years ago, in connection with the BBC Television children's programme *Wildtrack*, John Downer and I devised a simple pond which could be set up in even the smallest garden without too much effort. First of all you must choose the site very carefully: it needs to be level, and must be well away from trees so that it gets plenty of sunlight and does not become clogged with leaves in the autumn.

The materials required are as follows:

A pond liner, 8ft 3in × 6ft 6in (2.5m × 2m)
Ten wooden stakes
Mallet
Piece of timber, 6ft 6in × 2ft 6in × 2in (2m × 75cm × 50mm)
Spirit level
Spade
Some sand or old newspaper

The pond liner may be bought from a water garden or plastics supplier, but avoid anything less than 1000 gauge $^{15}/_{1000}$in (0.375 microns) thick as it is easily punctured. There are several kinds:

Black polythene – cheapest type, but has a limited life of about five years unless protected from sunlight by a covering of earth and stones. Use only water resistant type.

PVC sheeting – more expensive but more resistant to sunlight; best type is strengthened with nylon.

Polyolefin – a high-grade plastic liner with a life of over fifteen years.

Butyl rubber – a very flexible rubber liner with a life of over fifteen years. The best quality liner but the most expensive.

If you choose to line your pond with concrete it should be at least 6in (15cm) thick and must be sealed with bituminous paint or water-seal cement. But be warned that a concrete pond involves back-breaking work. Our advice is to plump for a Butyl liner, even though it is expensive.

METHOD
1 Mark out the edges of the pond with stakes; if the ground is not quite level, put the shallow end at the bottom of the slope. Hammer in a stake at each end of the pond using the

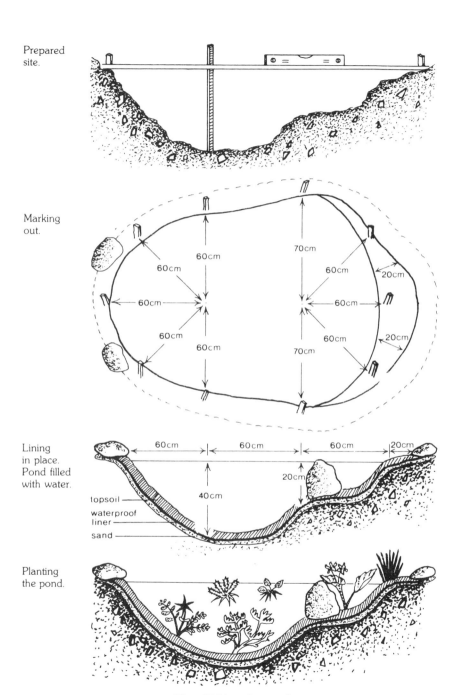

Prepared site.

Marking out.

60cm
60cm
60cm
60cm
70cm
60cm
20cm
60cm
70cm
60cm
20cm

Lining in place. Pond filled with water.

60cm
60cm
60cm
20cm
20cm
40cm
topsoil
waterproof liner
sand

Planting the pond.

The 'Wildtrack' pond

measurements on the diagram (see page 27; it is important to keep to these or the liner will not fit). Rest the wooden beam across the two stakes and mark a point on the beam 2ft (60cm) in from each stake. You can find the position of the other stakes by measuring out from these points.

2   You can now start to dig the pond. Put any turves to one side as you can use them later to fringe the pond. Save the topsoil as well, because this will be put back in the finished pond. The best of the soil could be used to make a bank. Put soil to one side, out of the way of the spread lining.

3   As soon as the hole begins to grow, check that the sides of the pond are at the same level by laying the wooden beam over the pond and checking with the spirit level. Take out the stakes and remove the earth from the higher sides.

4   Use the diagram to work out the different depths of the pond. The deepest part of the pond is a third of the way from the end, and the sides of the pond should shelve up gradually from this point to the edge. Do not make the slope too steep. Check the depths are right by measuring down from the wooden beam. If you dig too deep don't worry – you can always put some back!

5   A special feature of the pond is the marshy area at the shallow end. Extend it by removing earth to a depth of 2in (5cm) for a distance of 8in (20cm) away from that end.

6   When the hole is ready, pick out any stones or sticks which may puncture the lining and carefully pour in some damp sand to make a layer ¾in (2cm) deep over the whole of the pond. This is to give a soft base for the lining to rest on. If you prefer, you can use sheets of spread-out newspaper, but make sure you build up a good layer.

7   Take the liner, and with it overlap the deep end of the pond by 8in (20cm). Anchor it with heavy stones, temporarily.

8   Spread out the liner over the pond, and push it gently down into the hole. Don't try to make it fit too snugly as the weight of the water will do that.

9   Fill the pond almost to the top with water. You can now see whether you've made any mistakes in levelling the pond. Any errors can be put right by removing or adding earth under the liner. Make sure that there are going to be water levels of from ¾in to 4in (2cm to 10cm) at the shallow end.

10　You should wait two or three days to allow the liner to settle, then carefully trim off the surplus plastic round the edge leaving at least 8in (20cm) overlap, but do not cut any off the shallow end. Do not trim too soon as the weight of water drags in a lot of slack. And do not trim too close, or you will have difficulties when arranging your pond surround of stones or turf.

11　Secure the edges of the plastic by burying it under earth or large stones. You can also use the turf for this purpose. If you are using a polythene liner, it's very important to ensure the sheet is totally buried, as in time sunlight will destroy it.

12　Take the topsoil you have saved and sprinkle it over the surface of the pond until you have built up a layer of silt several inches deep over the liner. The earth will form a marshy area at the shallow end. This earth should not be in contact with the surrounding ground or in dry weather water will be drawn out of the pond.

13　Take a couple of large stones and carefully place them in the shallow end so that they show above the surface. Birds will use these as perching places.

Pond plants

The pond must be properly stocked with suitable plants for it to establish a healthy home for a living community. The plants release oxygen into the water and absorb the carbon dioxide produced by the water animals which are bound to colonise it. They also provide food, shade and shelter for the animals. They thrive on plenty of light, but welcome protection from strong winds. There are three main plant categories, and you should make certain your pond is stocked with some of each:

1　Free-floating plants live at the surface, with their roots suspended in the water, eg frogbit *Hydrocharis morus-ranae*; water soldier *Stratiotes aloides*; duckweed *Lemna sp.*; water violet *Hottonia palustris* – whose flowers are rich with nectar and attract pollinating insects.

2　Oxygenators live fully submerged in the deeper part of the pool, some rooted to the mud at the bottom. They are vital, eg starwort *Callitriche autumnalis*; millwort *Myriophyllum sp.*; hornwort *Ceratophyllum demersum*. The starwort is specially valuable because it retains its oxygenating properties throughout the winter. Quillwort *Isoetes lacustris*, is an excellent food plant from the point of view of fish.

3 Marginals live in marshy areas at the edge of the pond and have most of their foliage above water, eg water forget-me-not *Myosotis sp.*; brooklime *Veronica beccabunga*; marsh marigold *Caltha palustris*; flowering rush *Butomus umbellatus*; slender spike-rush *Eleocharis acicularis* (this may survive submerged but will then be sterile).

You can find these plants easily enough in wild ponds and ditches, but it is best to buy pest-free stock from a nurseryman (for address see page 32). Follow his instructions on planting, but a general rule is to put the marginals in water 1in to 4in (2.5cm to 10cm) deep, rooting them in good topsoil. The oxygenators will grow in water 6in to 24in (15cm to 60cm) deep; if they need planting (as *Myriophyllum*, for instance), the best method is to use the specially-made baskets which are cheap to buy and allow you to make subsequent gardening changes easily. A cheaper way is to take a piece of lead wire and bend it loosely around the base of the plant before you introduce it to a few inches of topsoil which covers the bottom of your pond.

Pond animals and visitors

Animals will find their own way to your pond, but it makes sense to introduce some common water snails straightaway, for they will serve a useful purpose in grazing the algae. Buy them from your aquarist, and remember that cheap ones eat just as efficiently as expensive ones. Ramshorn snails *Planorbis corneus*, or the freshwater winkle *Paludina vivipara*, are the species least likely to attack your 'best' plants. One snail to every 2sq in (5sq cm) of surface water is said to be the desired population, but don't put too many in, they will soon find their own balance.

You may wish to introduce frogs (by way of spawn clouds), toads (spawn strings), water spiders and beetles to suit your own whim. But go easy on the great diving beetle *Dytiscus marginalis*, if you are going to have largish fish because it will attack them. And avoid newts in a small pond for they will eat almost anything. Most insect species will find their own way – for instance dragonflies, water boatmen and pond skaters. Sticklebacks and minnows will control the mosquito and gnat larvae which will inevitably appear. Again, a rough rule of thumb is 1in (2.5cm) of fish to 24sq in (60sq cm) of surface area. On the whole it is probably best not to have any fish in a very small pond.

Birds will enjoy hunting the pond life, you will enjoy the drama. Robins and blackbirds go for tadpoles, blackbirds try for newts, kingfishers enjoy sticklebacks, and if you are un-British enough to introduce goldfish or carp, then you may be fortunate enough to be visited by a heron. But goldfish are a mixed blessing; they may look colourful but they are bottom feeders, creating in the process a continuous cloud of mud which means the water is rarely completely clear.

Theoretically, the pond should need little maintenance. When it is first filled and planted it will probably be opaque and green-looking for a while, but as the plants grow the water will clear. In hot weather you may well have to add water, especially if you are losing it by capillary action. Devise some way of trickle-feeding it, or diverting rain to it, to save a great deal of trouble. If it is near trees, then fallen leaves may

Anting starlings

need to be removed in the autumn, but it should not be necessary to clean the pond out. With well-balanced populations a pond will stay healthy for years.

You will find that the finished product will give you as much pond-watching pleasure as it does the birds and if, one day, a heron comes and eats your fish you must grin and bear it and re-stock the pond.

It really isn't possible, or natural, to try to run a sort of 'paradise garden' in which predators have no place. However hard it may be for us to reconcile ourselves to it, the fact is that predators like foxes, sparrowhawks and herons, which prey on and eat other species, are operating in the best interests of the species on which they prey. By catching the slower individuals which are off-colour or sick, they are continually weeding out the less healthy members of a species so that it is the fittest which survive. So please do try to understand both sides of the argument. When the magpie eats eggs or small birds it is doing its job as a magpie, not acting like a pantomime villain!

Unless your garden is on sandy ground, you may like to provide a dust bath for sparrows and wrens. The dusting-place should be well sheltered, with some cover nearby, and can consist of a couple of square feet of well-sifted sand, earth and ash to a depth of a few inches. Sprinkle the dust bath with bug powder or spray (eg Cooper's Household Insect Powder or Poultry Aerosol) every now and again, for the common good. Birds will also sun-bathe, smoke-bathe, and even bathe in ants, all strange manifestations of the need to maintain feather performance at peak efficiency.

Suppliers of pond plants, etc
Griffin & George Ltd, Gerrard Biological Centre, The Field Station, Beam Brook, Newdigate, Dorking, Surrey RH5 5EF. Suppliers of pond plants and animals. Send for lists.

Queensborough Fisheries, 111 Goldhawk Road, Shepherds Bush, London W12 8EJ. Send for list.

The London Aquatic Co Ltd, 42 Finsbury Road, Wood Green, London N22 4PD. Illustrated catalogue.

3   Nest sites and nestboxes

When your garden is stocked with welcoming berry-laden shrubs and a drinking pool, the next move is to induce some of your bird visitors to go the whole hog and take up permanent residence. By their nature houses, outbuildings and gardens provide dozens of potential nest sites, although in these tidy-minded days we tend to build with fewer holes and corners. Very often, we can turn an uninviting building into a highly-desirable bird residence with the minimum of effort. Once again, we must bear in mind that different birds have different requirements, and while a blue tit will choose a secret place, entered by what seems an impossibly narrow hole, a swan will build a great mound of a nest and sit in state for all to see. In many coastal areas we have the curious spectacle of herring gulls choosing to nest on rooftops and by chimney pots.

We can divide birds roughly into those which nest in holes and those which do not. Tits, nuthatches, tree-sparrows, redstarts and woodpeckers are hole-nesters, while spotted flycatchers, robins, blackbirds and thrushes live mostly on the open plan. All birds, no matter what type of nest they choose, need protection from their enemies and shelter from the elements if they are to thrive, so most of them build in cover of some kind.

Natural nest sites

Hedges are the most obvious places for nests. A good beech, holly, hawthorn or yew hedge contains dozens of likely building sites and also provides a good defence barrier. It is important that there should be plenty of forks in the branches to provide a foundation for the first nest twigs. (Hazel makes a poor nesting tree because it offers so few fork sites.) By judicious pruning at about the 5ft (1.5m) height you can often turn an unpromising hedge into a likely attraction. Prune your hedge in early spring and autumn, leaving it undisturbed during the breeding season. When pruning fruit trees, make a crotch-site here and there in the body of the tree, in the hope of attracting a goldfinch to nest.

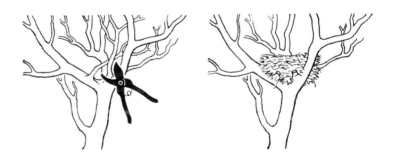

The berry-bearing shrubs often serve as nesting areas in the spring; if you have brambles and gorse in your garden, you may find they will harbour dunnocks or linnets. Honeysuckle seems to have a special attraction for flycatchers. Once a bird has chosen its nest site leave it to get on with the job. Don't try to help it with the construction, and don't 'improve' the situation, or it may desert. Don't fuss it!

A friend of mine who made an island on his pond was

rewarded by having a pair of Canada geese take it over. If you are lucky enough to have plenty of water, grow a lush area of wild celery, millet, reeds and sedges in clumps. If the reed-bed is large enough, you may get reed and sedge warblers, and possibly reed buntings, building in it.

Now for the hole-nesters. Naturally, they will prefer tree holes and it may be that you already have some old trees – fruit trees, perhaps – which have begun to decay in a manner attractive to birds. If not, you might consider introducing some holes into a decaying tree with a brace and bit. Start some promising holes of about 1¼in (32mm) diameter and a woodpecker may finish the job. If the woodpecker gives up, a nuthatch may take over and plaster the entrance hole with mud to suit its own preference. Or, you might try importing an old tree or tree trunk, complete with holes, and setting it up in a secluded position. At worst, you will end up with a pair of starlings. Personally, I like to have a pair of starlings nesting nearby because they are such entertaining vocalists and are remarkable mimics. We once had one that gave a first-class rendering of a hen that had just laid an egg, but the climax of its repertoire was a beautiful pussy-cat's miaow.

Making and enlarging holes is great fun, and when you have finished working on trees, you might turn your attentions to the walls of your house and outbuildings. Quite often it is possible to enlarge cracks so that there is the 1⅛in necessary for a tit to squeeze through. I am not suggesting you tear your house apart just for a few birds, but you will find plenty of likely and safe places if you look around, armed with a strong auger or jemmy. Try drilling some discreet 1¼in (32mm) holes in your garage doors. Make one entrance up near the roof and swallows may colonise the loft, although you will need to have a ceiling to protect the cellulose of your car from the droppings.

If you are building a garden wall, do not overdo the pointing; leave one or two gaps and you may attract a pied wagtail. Even grey wagtails take freely to man-provided nest sites in culvert and bridge stonework. The height of the holes and cavities is not vitally important, although round about the 5ft (1.5m) mark is probably ideal. With a desirable site, birds will not be too choosy. Robins have nested at ground level and great tits as high as 24ft (7.2m), although these are

35

exceptional instances. The holes should, however, be in a sheltered position and facing somewhere within an arc drawn from north through east to south-east. Hot sun is bad, and so is an entrance facing into a cold wind. Heat, especially, can easily kill young nestlings when they become exhausted.

An ancient, disintegrating stone wall is an asset to cherish and so is an old garden shed. The wall may be a haven for tits, nuthatches and wagtails, and the shed may be a thriving bird slum in no time at all if you develop it a little. Shelves around the walls and under the roof at different heights could provide homes for swallows, blackbirds and robins. A bundle of pea sticks in a corner may make a home for a wren. Leave an old tweed coat hanging up with a wide pocket gaping open for a robin. Keep the floor clear, though, to discourage rats. If necessary, put a rat-trap tunnel against the walls, but see that it does not let in light and attract ground birds. Make sure there is a good entrance hole somewhere, in case a bird is locked in by mistake.

On the outside of the shed grow a jungle of creeping ivy and honeysuckle, for it may well entice a robin to build. Hide a half-coconut (with a drain-hole in the bottom of the cup) in the creeper for a possible spotted flycatcher. Try excavating a nest cavity in the middle of a brushwood bundle and lean it against an outside wall. Lastly, lean an old plank against the dampest, darkest wall to make a haven for snails, and farm them on behalf of the thrushes.

Man-made nest sites

There is good historical precedent for putting up bird houses (Noah had a dove-cote on top of the Ark). In Roman times there was a thriving pigeon 'fancy' with rooftop pigeon towns. Columbaria of differing architectural styles spread from Rome through Europe to Scotland and the rest of Britain through the centuries. The custom declined in the eighteenth century, when the introduction of root and clover crops made it possible to keep more cattle and sheep through the winter, thus providing fresh meat which made the pigeon 'squab' redundant.

In the Middle Ages clay flasks and wooden boxes were used to attract small birds to nest, in order that the resulting fat juveniles could be taken for food. Probably the first man to use nestboxes simply for the pleasure of encouraging birds to nest was the eccentric Yorkshire naturalist Charles Waterton, in the early nineteenth century.

But the traditional back-garden nestbox is the robin's kettle, stuck 5ft (1.5m) up in the fork of a tree. The kettle should be at least quart size, and the spout should point down so that rainwater can drain away. As an encouragement, prime the nest with some dead leaves or a plaited circle of straw.

The most unusual man-made nest site I ever saw was a birdcage, hanging high up on a cob wall in the village of Middle Wallop in Hampshire. It turned out that a hoopoe had reared young in a perfectly normal cavity-site in the wall, but one of the nestlings had fallen out of the hole a bit too soon. The villagers had hoisted up the birdcage and left the door open, installing the unfortunate young bird inside. Incredibly, the adult hoopoe carried on feeding the baby as if nothing had happened, going in and out of the birdcage as if it were the most ordinary thing in the world. The story has a happy ending too, because the whole family finally fledged success-fully and flew off. But hoopoes are rare breeders in this country, so I am not going to suggest that we all invest in hoopoe birdcages.

Every year for some time past a pair of mute swans has tried to nest on a tidal sandbank near the mouth of the estuary at Newton Ferrers in South Devon. They seem unable to grasp the fact that Atlantic seawater rises and falls, and as fast as they build a nest the rising tide washes it away. The scientists of the International Paint Company, who have a research station nearby, came to the rescue, constructing a special swan raft on empty 5gal oil drums. They anchored it in position and piled the beginning of a swan's nest onto it. The swans took it over and now every year they complete their nest, lay eggs, brood and hatch the cygnets; every time the tide comes in, the nest and contents rise gently and float, serene and safe.

Rafts have also been used successfully to encourage wild ducks, great-crested grebes, common terns, greylag and Canada geese, moorhens and coots. Their great advantage is that they give a degree of safety from land-borne predators, but they are easier to write about than to construct. They consist of a platform supported by buoyancy tanks, 40gal drums or steel tanks, held by a framework of timber or angle iron. The platform, or deck, should be devised to carry a layer of soil or shingle stabilised with suitable plants; polythene sheeting will help to retain sufficient rain water to keep the soil wet. Make sure that there is a ramp or some sort of suitable access point so that the birds can launch themselves into the water and get back onto the raft easily.

In the Dee estuary, common terns have successfully colonised a raft moored on a reservoir belonging to the British Steel Corporation. The raft, constructed by the Merseyside Ringing Group, was a massive affair of telegraph poles decked with railway sleepers, covered with slag, shingle and grass sods. Blocks of expanded polystyrene provided the buoyancy and the resulting 'floating island' was 100sq ft (30sq m), taking the weight of three men with ease. Secured by nylon lines to scrap-iron anchors, this incongruous device floated serenely in a scene characterised by slag tips, blast furnaces, power stations, and the constant disturbance of a modern steel works. Yet the terns arriving in spring from their West African wintering grounds took up residence and successfully defended their new territory against the attentions of herring gulls.

As the months went by a colony of terns became established, and in that first year the Merseyside group ringed sixteen young birds. In this way, what had been a steady decline in numbers at the nearby old-established ternery was halted, and it is hoped that the Dee tern colony will soon be up to its former strength. A fine example of the way in which intelligent interpretation of a species' needs may help to maintain it in adverse conditions.

All over Europe there are traditions which have led people to encourage birds to adopt man-made nest sites. In many villages in Germany, a cartwheel is fixed to the top of a high pole in the hope of attracting a stork to nest. And in Switzerland and Holland they have developed a successful pole-top nestbox for kestrels. If you have a large secluded garden in good kestrel country (and this includes cities), you might consider the experiment of putting up one of these boxes. Farmers who are bothered with mice might also think it worth the effort. (Constructional details are given on page 108.) Kestrels are among those species which have learned to take advantage of the urban life. Back in 1971 a kestrel family successfully used a window-box on the sixteenth floor of a twenty-storey block of flats at Peckham, London. Two chicks were fledged on a diet of house sparrows. The owner of the flat found the birds too messy for her comfort, and boarded up the ledge, but the hawks were undismayed, nesting successfully the following year on the nearest suitable tower block, in Southwark. Nowadays kestrels breed freely in towns.

There are two basic types of nestbox: an enclosed space with a small entrance hole, and a tray or ledge with or without sides and roof. They can be readily obtained at reasonable prices (suppliers' addresses are given on page 79–82) or you may prefer to make your own; there is an extra satisfaction in seeing birds take over a nestbox you have built with your own hands. The method of construction will be discussed here in general terms, as the type of box and critical

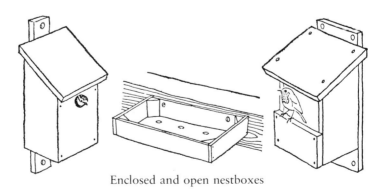

Enclosed and open nestboxes

sizes for each species will be found listed in the notes in Chapter 6. The nesthole measurement most people want to know straightaway is one which excludes starlings and sparrows. The answer is 1⅛in (29mm). This will give entry to all the tits, and nuthatches, but also tree sparrows, which may not be quite so welcome. Starlings cannot manage a hole smaller than 1½in diameter, and house sparrows are deterred by holes under 1¼in (32mm). But they have a disconcerting habit of trying hard even if they can't get in, and may prevent other species gaining access simply by laying claim to the site and poking nest material into the hole. The hole-type of nestbox is usually the most successful, because it reproduces the type of nest site which is harder to find round the average house, and also because suburban birds tend to be woodland species which are largely hole-in-tree nesters.

But remember that blackbirds, pied wagtails and robins, for instance, live on the 'open plan' and need a very large entrance. So make boxes of both types.

Although at first sight it may seem that the 'rustic' type of nestbox will be most suitable I think the plain kind is preferable; the birds certainly do not seem to mind one way or the other, so the main criteria are construction and amenity. The plain square types are undoubtedly easiest to make, and I think they look most attractive. The 'rustic' boxes are usually made of birch. If they were only fixed to birch trees I should have no objection, but this is seldom the case. Birch boxes attached to oak or beech or elm trees make rather an unhappy and unnatural contrast. Perhaps there is some case for using rustic boxes when it is important that they should not be too easily discovered, in public places for instance, but I think it is a weak one. Small boys on the warpath will discover either type in no time, and if this is a danger the boxes should be fixed high, say not less than 12ft (3.6m).

The boxes should be made of ¾in (20mm) wood, which will stand up to weathering for a reasonable time and be thick enough to insulate the interior temperature from violent changes. Hardwood is most suitable as it is more resistant to weather than softwood. Seasoned oak is probably the best, although it is hard to cut and may split. Of the softwoods, cedar is very satisfactory and weathers nicely. Second-hand floor boarding serves well, and is often exactly the right size

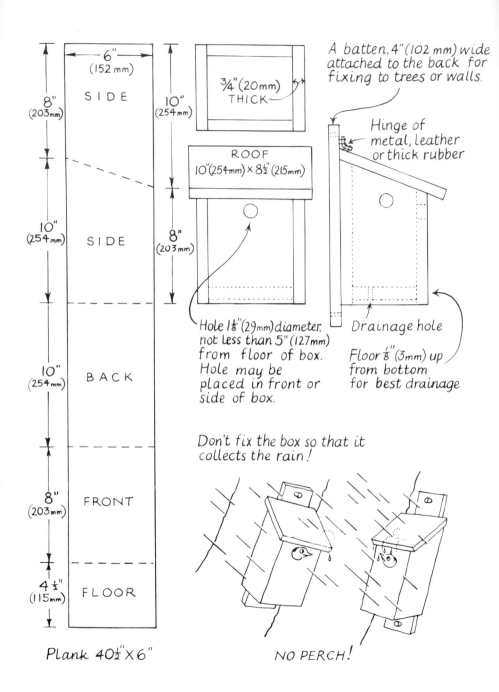

6"
(152 mm)

SIDE

8"
(203mm)

10"
(254mm)

10"
(254mm)

SIDE

8"
(203mm)

3/4" (20mm)
THICK

ROOF
10"(254mm) × 8½" (215mm)

A batten, 4" (102 mm) wide
attached to the back for
fixing to trees or walls.

Hinge of
metal, leather
or thick rubber

10"
(254mm)

BACK

Hole 1⅛"(29mm) diameter,
not less than 5" (127mm)
from floor of box.
Hole may be
placed in front or
side of box.

Drainage hole

Floor ⅛" (3mm) up
from bottom
for best drainage

8"
(203mm)

FRONT

Don't fix the box so that it
collects the rain!

4½"
(115mm)

FLOOR

Plank 40½"× 6"

NO PERCH!

Construction details for a basic titbox

for the job. You can get it, sometimes for the asking, from any building site where they are renovating old houses.

It is important that the box should not warp and so allow wind and rain to attack the nestlings. One side may be removable for cleaning purposes, but make sure that it fits firmly in position when in use and that there is no danger of it falling out and exposing the nest to predators. Make sure, too, that the roof fits flush to the walls so that the box is as watertight as possible, and also that the roof overlaps the outside edges so that rain drips clear.

Seal the wall joints with a sealing compound, such as Seelastic or Bostik, before you finally nail or screw the pieces into position (using galvanised nails).

Many nestlings drown in natural nest sites and we should take particular care to exclude rain when we invite birds to use the boxes we provide. The entrance hole should be at the top of the box, otherwise a cat may be able to fish the young birds out, or they may be seen by other predators when they stretch up to beg for food. The inside floor measurements must allow birds plenty of room to stretch their growing wings. Make a ventilation and drainage hole in the floor, since some birds are not too particular about their nest sanitation. The better you make the box the more important is the drain hole.

It isn't necessary to paint the finished box, but a coat of creosote will increase its probable lifespan. *Audubon Magazine*, in the United States, reported an eleven-year study in which a whole range of coloured nestboxes was offered to birds, in order to see if they had preferences. Of 98 used boxes, 41 were red, 31 green, 16 blue, 8 yellow, 2 white. They don't seem to have offered black ones, which would probably have been unpopular, and it is a pity they didn't offer natural wood and creosoted wood for comparison. Anyway, it's clear that you should avoid yellow or white! If you *change* colour, birds will take a little time to accept that change, because it induces a 'scared' response similar to that produced by a predator.

Ideally the nextboxes should be fixed in position in October or November. This gives them a chance to weather into their surroundings, and their potential occupiers have plenty of time to get used to them and to explore their possibilities. It

may well be that they will be used during the winter months as a roost box. There is an astonishing account, by experienced nestbox watchers in Norfolk, of a box with an interior space of 4½in × 5½in × 5¾in (11.3cm × 13.8cm × 14.5cm) being occupied at night by over sixty wrens, huddled together for winter warmth and occupying 2.33 cubic inches per body! Female blue tits often roost in deep winter in the box which they will use for nesting in spring.

Nestboxes may, of course, be put up at any time in the winter, but if you are hoping they will be occupied in their first spring, they ought to be up by the end of February. However, better late than never, especially if there's a shortage of natural sites, and there are plenty of records of boxes being occupied within days of erection.

The boxes can be fixed at a height of about 6ft (1.8m), though this is not the most important factor. The position should be protected from prevailing cold winds and shaded from the hot sun: as already mentioned, the box should face somewhere in the arc from north through east to south-east. The location should not be thickly sheltered or darkened by foliage, and the adult birds should have a fairly clear flight path to and from the nest. A convenient staging post should be available, some 6ft (1.8m) away.

The entrance hole must be far enough from its fixing wall or tree trunk to allow the incoming bird to have fully-stretched wings till the last moment before landing. Don't have a landing perch attached to the box, as this may provide a cat or a squirrel with a good position for extracting the babies. Your birds certainly don't need the perch to help them enter the box. If you want a perch for photographic purposes put it several feet away. The birds will probably be glad to use it as a staging-post.

The box should be fixed in such a way that the top of the entrance hole wall is inclined outwards to exclude rain, and it should be secured to its anchorage by means of a batten, so that it does not become waterlogged where attached to the wall or trunk. It is not important to fix the box rigidly although obviously it is vital that it doesn't fall down. From the bird's point of view, a box which swings in the wind is no more than the artificial version of a swaying branch. Use copper nails when fixing the box to a tree, if there is any chance that the tree may be subsequently felled for timber. It will be kinder to the saw blade.

Do not have a nestbox close to a bird table, because the 'owners' will object to the continual coming and going of visitors to the feeding station and there will be a lot of wasted effort in trying to see them off.

Do not put up too many boxes too close together: like some of us, some birds prefer to keep their distance from each other (although this does not apply to colonial nesters like martins). Many species with a strong territorial instinct like to 'own' their plot but, fortunately, they do not as a rule object to members of other species living nearby. Thus robins, which have a highly-developed sense of territory, will not object to tits as close neighbours. It is difficult to say how many boxes should be erected because so many factors are involved, but where there is a large area to cover it is probably worth trying a dozen to the acre; more if the area is drastically short of natural nest sites. Put up twice as many enclosed boxes as open ones. If there are good natural or semi-natural sites available it may be that the boxes will be ignored altogether. On the other hand, blue tits may inspect, 'buy' and start building within a day of erection.

Open-plan boxes should be fixed in suitable crotch-sites in trees and bushes, and cunningly hidden in ivy or creeper-clad walls. However cleverly you may hide them away you can be quite certain the birds will find them without any delay.

One more thing will help make your boxes attractive. Put a shallow layer of moss, or thin plaited straw, in the bottom of boxes destined for passerines. If you are hoping for a woodpecker, try priming the box with a sprinkling of sawdust or chippings and, as an appetizer, a few beetles and grubs. In early spring, when the birds are beginning to build, they will be searching everywhere for nesting materials. Jackdaws will take paper bags from litter-bins, or perch on a horse's back to steal hairs. When I was on the Galápagos Islands I once found a cormorant's nest that had a boat's rowlock ingeniously woven into the structure.

Birds are more than willing to be helped with their search for construction materials. Straw, feathers, dog or cat combings, short bits of cotton, cotton wool, sheep wool and poultry down (after treatment with bug-powder) are all grist to their mill. Stuff them in two mesh bags – hanging one from the bird table or branch and pegging the other to the ground for ground-birds. It is safest to offer dull-coloured materials, but there is nothing more charming than a sitting bird surrounded by a delicate garnish of coloured cottons. A naturalist once took a sparrow's nest to pieces and found it consisted of 1,282 separate items, which included 1,063 pieces of dead grass, 126 strips of bark, 15 pieces of paper, 10 pieces of cellophane, 13 pieces of tissue, 25 pieces of cotton thread, 28 wild bird feathers, one piece of string and a cotton bandage. The disadvantage of these exhibitionist nests is that they are somewhat conspicuous, and may attract predators. On the other hand evidence suggests that in some species the cock bird deliberately imports decorations which enhance his courting status.

Woodpeckers or sparrows may 'improve' a nestbox, and in one case a squirrel was reported to have enlarged a small hole to 2½in (63mm) diameter. Having gained entrance, the intruder may well eat the young chicks it finds inside. To foil this activity, the RSPB makes a metal plate, with a tit-size hole in it, which can be fixed over the vulnerable wood. But even a vandalised box may produce happy results, for a nuthatch may come along and plaster the edges of the hole to suit its own requirements.

Both great and blue tits will sometimes peck at the entrance holes to their boxes, but this is perfectly normal behaviour; it is not their way of telling you that the hole is too small.

Never alter the position of a box after a bird has adopted it, and never disturb the bird when it is sitting. You will often hear people speak of the tameness of sitting birds; the truth is that the brooding instinct is stronger than the bird's terror of being close to a human. The privacy of a bird's nest should be respected and we should neither fuss nor photograph without good reason.

And when, at last, your nestbox contains a noisy, struggling muddle of baby birds, try to contain yourself and do not peer in too often. Examine the box every two or three days, and only when the adult bird is not at home. Nothing disconcerts a wild bird quite so much as the sudden appearance of a vast human face inches away from it. Be particularly careful not to cause nearly-fledged birds to leave the nest too soon. This is a critical time, and it would be a disaster if the brood 'exploded' into the world before their time. If you inadvertently cause the young birds to fly, collect them up carefully and 'post' them back into the box. Stuff the entrance hole with a handkerchief for ten minutes or so. And then when the panic has subsided, remove the handkerchief very, very gently.

All birds are attacked by parasites such as fleas, lice and bird flies, so after the young have flown from the box (and remember it may serve for two or more broods) it should be cleaned out and given a dose of a pyrethrum-based bug killer, eg Cooper's Poultry Aerosol and re-creosoted. If you now prime the de-loused box with a thin layer of moss it will, perhaps, serve for a second brood or be ready later on for use as a winter roost box.

Incidentally, don't be too sad if when you come to clean

out your box you find one or two eggs that did not hatch, or even one or two dead young. This is a common enough occurrence, possibly due to a shortage of food at a critical time, but it is part of the natural course of events. If every blue tit egg developed into an adult blue tit, there very soon wouldn't be room on planet earth for any of the rest of us.

Much of the ornithologist's knowledge and understanding of the various stages of the breeding cycle in hole-nesting birds comes from nestbox studies. The British Trust for Ornithology has for years been recording nestbox information on special cards, which are subsequently analysed in computer fashion, but they are careful to insist that the interests of the birds comes before the importance of the card. If you would like to join in with this important work, contact the BTO (see address page 168). And you will certainly want to get hold of the Trust's excellent field guide, *Nestboxes*, by Chris du Feu. It is the definitive book on nestboxes, written for research workers who use them for bird breeding studies. And for a fascinating study of birds in gardens read *The Garden Bird Book*, edited by David Glue for the BTO and published by Macmillan, 1982.

Lifespans of wild birds

These figures show the *maximum recorded* lifespan in the wild for an individual of each species (to the nearest year); the *average* life expectancy for wild birds is, of course, very short indeed. These are records of the exceptional individual which has managed to survive against all the odds. The figures are available as a result of the international bird-ringing schemes which have been in operation for many years now with the object of learning more about bird numbers and migrations.

If you come across a bird with a ring on its leg, send full details (ring number, date, place, species of bird, whether the bird is freshly dead or not, or if it was alive and subsequently released, and any other relevant information) to the British Trust for Ornithology, (address page 168). In due course you will be told the place and date of its original ringing.

Pigeon rings should be sent to the Royal Pigeon Racing Association, The Reddings, Cheltenham, Glos GL51 6RN.

Note: The bracketed figures are certainly unrealistic. The species involved have not been ringed in large numbers and the recovery results have yet to reveal a long-lived individual.

Blackbird	20	Gull, Herring	20
Blackcap	7	Hawfinch	7
Brambling	7	Heron, Grey	18
Bullfinch	9	Hoopoe	(2)
Chaffinch	12	Jackdaw	14
Crossbill	(2)	Jay	15
Dipper	8	Kestrel	16
Dove, Collared	13	Kingfisher	4
Dove, Rock	6	Kittiwake	23
Dove, Stock	9	Magpie	9
Dunnock	9	Mallard	20
Eider	24	Martin, House	6
Fieldfare	9	Martin, Sand	8
Flycatcher, Pied	7	Moorhen	11
Flycatcher, Spotted	9	Nuthatch	8
Goldcrest	4	Owl, Barn	13
Goldfinch	7	Owl, Little	9
Goose, Canada	17	Owl, Tawny	16
Greenfinch	11	Pheasant	9
Gull, Black-headed	21	Pigeon, Wood	16

Blue tits. Only five nestlings in this box, but there could be as many as fourteen! The neat nest cup is soon abandoned and the material trodden into the floor of the box (*OSF/Bruce Coleman Ltd*)

Spotted flycatchers decorate a flower basket; ideally it should be hidden away in dense honeysuckle, and there should be a convenient perch a few feet away (*Brian Hawkes/NHPA*)

Pigeons were one of the earliest birds to be encouraged to use artificial nestboxes, but their squabs were destined for the pot; farmhouse dovecote in south-west France (*Tony Soper*)

Pipit, Rock	9	Tit, Coal	7
Redstart	8	Tit, Crested	5
Redstart, Black	5	Tit, Great	9
Redwing	6	Tit, Long-tailed	8
Robin	8	Tit, Marsh	9
Rook	18	Tit, Willow	8
Shelduck	14	Treecreeper	7
Siskin	7	Turnstone	14
Starling	20	Wagtail, Grey	6
Sparrow, House	12	Wagtail, Pied	10
Sparrow, Tree	7	Wheatear	7
Sparrowhawk	10	Woodpecker, Great	
Swallow	16	Spotted	10
Swan, Mute	22	Woodpecker, Green	5
Swift	15	Wren	5
Thrush, Mistle	8	Wryneck	4
Thrush, Song	10	Yellowhammer	9
Tit, Blue	12		

Birds which use nestboxes, ledges or rafts . . .

Blackbird	Flycatcher, Pied
Blackcap	Flycatcher, Spotted
Brambling	Fulmar
Bullfinch	Gadwall
Bunting, Reed	Goldcrest
Bunting, Snow	Goldeneye
Chaffinch	Goldfinch
Chiffchaff	Goose, Canada
Chough	Goose, Greylag
Coot	Grebe, Great Crested
Crossbill	Greenfinch
Dipper	Gull, Black-headed
Diver, Black-throated	Gull, Herring
Dove, Collared	Hawfinch
Dove, Rock	Heron, Grey
Dove, Stock	Hoopoe
Duck, Tufted	Jackdaw
Dunnock	Jay
Eider	Kestrel
Fieldfare	Kingfisher
Firecrest	Linnet

Magpie
Mallard
Mandarin
Martin, House
Martin, Sand
Moorhen
Nuthatch
Osprey
Owl, Barn
Owl, Little
Owl, Long-eared
Owl, Tawny
Pheasant
Pigeon, Wood
Pipit, Meadow
Pipit, Rock
Redpoll
Redstart
Redstart, Black
Redwing
Robin
Rook
Skylark
Shelduck
Siskin
Sparrowhawk
Sparrow, House

Sparrow, Tree
Starling
Swallow
Swan, Mute
Swift
Tern, Common
Thrush, Mistle
Thrush, Song
Tit, Blue
Tit, Coal
Tit, Crested
Tit, Great
Tit, Long-tailed
Tit, Marsh
Tit, Willow
Treecreeper
Turnstone
Wagtail, Pied
Waxwing
Wheatear
Woodpecker, Great Spotted
Woodpecker, Green
Woodpecker, Lesser Spotted
Wren
Wryneck
Yellowhammer

The British Trust for Ornithology runs a Nest Record Scheme, in which the object is to collect information about the breeding behaviour of British birds. If you feel you could collect simple, but precise, information about the birds which nest in your garden, and not necessarily in nestboxes, write to the BTO (address page 168) for information.

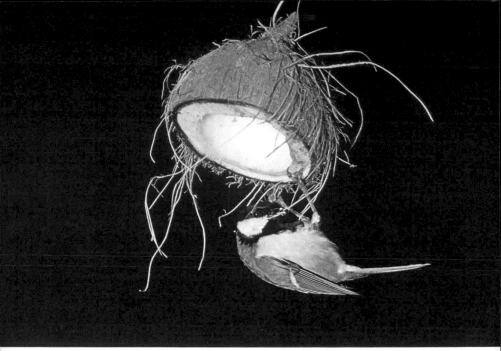

Half coconuts provide good fatty food and only the more acrobatic birds, like this great tit, can get at it (*Walter Murray/NHPA*)

Robins are easily tamed by way of their stomachs – they like mealworms a lot (*John Markham/Bruce Coleman Ltd*)

Swallow at nest with young; one chick is gaping for food (*Inigo Everson/Bruce Coleman Ltd*)

4   *The bird table*

Housed in comfort and surrounded by a garden which provides them with worms, berries and fresh water, your birds have little to complain about. But if you are prepared to go one step further, you can give yourself a great deal of extra pleasure. By providing food you can entice the birds to show themselves more freely in places where you can watch them. And, as the availability of food controls to some extent the bird population of your garden, you will also be increasing their numbers. But providing food is not a pleasure to undertake lightly. Put out some scraps in the garden and you will very soon attract new residents. They will become dependent on your generosity, and if it fails they will be competing for an inadequate supply of natural foods. Especially in cold weather birds may lose a lot of weight overnight, and they have to make it up again during the brief hours of daylight. Death comes in a matter of hours even to a healthy small bird, if it is without food. In hard weather the real killer is hunger, not cold.

The problems are simple enough to list: what to provide,

and how to serve it? You may think it sufficient simply to throw bread scraps onto the lawn, but this will not do at all. Bread alone, especially mass-produced white bread, is about as good for birds as it is for us, and certainly does not constitute a satisfactory diet. Besides, some birds do not care to come down to ground level for their food; in any case there is always the threat of a cat waiting in the wings! Again some birds are carnivorous and others vegetarian. It is no good offering a snail to a chaffinch, or a sunflower seed to a wren. A quick glance at a bird's bill will give a clue to its diet. Finches have nutcracker bills, adapted to crack and crush, and they feed mostly on grain and seeds. They are hard-billed birds. In the other basic category, soft-bills, we have, for instance, robins and wrens with slender bills adapted to deal with grubs, caterpillars and other insects.

Natural food

The best food to provide is what the birds would choose for themselves. One way to do this is to go on a nut and berry collecting expedition in the autumn. From August to October, you will be able to collect a fine harvest along the hedgerows. Pick the berries when they are just ripe.

In August your target should be the rowan. Later on, elderberries are first-quality bird food. Rowan and elder are probably the best berries, but wild cherry and haws are also good. Sloes do not seem to be very much liked by birds, nor are blackberries very popular. Crab apples are worth collecting, and in a bad winter you will find fieldfares coming to the bird table for them. As for nuts, the best choice is the hazel, but almonds are also very useful, especially for pleasing great spotted woodpeckers. Collect conkers and sweet chestnuts, acorns and beechmast from the ground as soon as they have fallen.

Dry the berries, and store both berries and nuts in a dry, dark place, and they will keep until you need them. Use shallow trays and arrange the fruits in a single layer. Gather pine and larch cones and take out the seeds from between the woody scales. Store all seeds including weed-seeds such as thistle, knapweed, teazle, ragwort and stinging-nettle, in muslin bags, hung up where the air can get at them. In severe weather when the ground is hard with frost, take a spade and

The best bird tables are easy to clean and offer the food some protection from rain (*Walter Murray/NHPA*)

The RSPB scrap feeder is ideal for peanuts and much appreciated by great and blue tits among others (*Eric Hasking*)

Like many birds which normally nest in tree holes, stock doves will take over a box, but they need a somewhat bigger entrance hole than blue tits (*Mike Read/Swift Picture Library*)

turn some earth over. This will provide a much-needed supplement to the bird-table food.

Kitchen scraps

Many people will tell you that birds love bread, and though this is true, nobody would suggest that bread alone provides a balanced diet. It is better than nothing and wholemeal is better than white, but it is a poor substitute for a varied selection of more nutritious food. One of the most popular bird table foods is uncooked pastry, with the advantage that it can be moulded into all sorts of odd cracks and crannies round the bird table.

Potato, especially baked in the jacket, is a useful staple. Stale cake is good, especially if home made with a high protein content. Minced raw meat, meat bones, cooked and chopped bacon rinds and cheese are all good. An excellent use for fat is as a binding material for bird-pudding – the best kitchen scrap bird offering of all, for which some recipes are given on page 77. Almost everything except highly-seasoned or salty food can go into the basket for bird kitchen scraps. Be careful to exclude salt though, for it will kill most small birds. But on the whole you don't need to worry about giving birds something that may disagree with them; they will select what suits them and leave the rest. One way and another, you will not find much is wasted. But be careful with cooked bones which may be taken by dogs (or foxes) when splinters may become stuck in their guts.

If you have one of those splendid whole Stilton cheeses at Christmas, don't throw away the near-empty shell when it is finished. Birds are very partial to Stilton, but prefer it when it

is not swamped with port! Melon seeds can be another exotic bird table success.

Specially-bought food

There are several firms producing bird food (see list on page 78) and, if you can stand the expense, this is certainly an easy way to solve the supply problem. John Haith Ltd, of Cleethorpes, for instance, produce a 'wild bird food' which caters for most tastes. With mixed seeds, especially sunflower seeds, and peanut kernels, your birds will be well served.

Peanuts are, without a doubt, a 'best buy'. They are full of calories, convenient to handle, store and serve. Unshelled, they can be strung up to serve as playthings for tits and nuthatches. Other nuts are all worth buying. Nuthatches, in particular, love brazils. Coconut is good, but serve it in the shell (sawn in half and suspended so that rain can't get in), not desiccated or ground, as this will swell up inside a bird's stomach with dire results. It is especially important not to offer ground coconut in the breeding season, when it may be fed too generously to juvenile tits. Generally speaking, there should be enough natural food available for birds during the late spring and summer, and it is unwise to feed freely, if at all. Peanuts, for instance, cannot be digested by young nestling tits. I don't know whether coconut juice is good for birds, but you might like to experiment. Starlings love milk, and so do tits.

Mixed wild-bird seed can be bought from pet shops. But the most welcome seed, which nuthatches love, is hemp. Split some for the smaller birds, or buy it in crushed form.

Sunflower, canary, millet, maize, oats and corn are all good. Coarse oatmeal from chain-stores should be offered raw, as porridge is too glutinous and sticks to plumage and bill. Rice, on the other hand, should be boiled before you serve it.

You may be able to arrange with your local fruiterer for a box of unsaleable fruit to be kept aside for you. Apples, oranges, tomatoes, grapefruit, bananas and grapes are all equally acceptable if you just cut them up. In hard times, birds will eat this fruit ravenously, and in very cold weather suet may usefully be added because it provides energy so efficiently. Great spotted woodpeckers are especially fond of suet, which you can cram into the odd cranny.

For live insect food, the best buys are mealworms and ants' eggs. Robins are mad about mealworms. You can buy them direct from pet shops or bird-food suppliers, or you can breed them yourself. (Addresses on page 78.)

Mealworm culture

Take a smooth-sided container such as a large circular biscuit tin or one of those out-dated and highly unsuitable glass bowls traditionally used for unfortunate goldfish. An open top provides plenty of air, but have a wire mesh lid which will foil escape attempts.

Peanuts have helped to fuel the siskin's spread to southern Britain (*S. G. Porter/Bruce Coleman Ltd*)

Thrushes, like this fieldfare, much enjoy windfall fruit in winter (*Mike Read/Swift Picture Library*)

Put a 4in to 6in (10cm to 15cm) layer of dry wheat bran or barley meal in the bottom. Now a layer of hessian sacking. Add a vegetable layer of carrot, turnip, banana and apple skins, dry bread, raw potato, cabbage, as available – but ensure that the medium does not become too wet as it will then ferment, smell appalling and probably kill the mealworms. A good productive mixture will not smell. Then take more hessian sacking and add more vegetable/bran layers to produce a multi-tier sandwich of mealworm delight. Introduce 200–300 mealworms (mealworms from an aviculturist's pet shop, *not* an angler's maggots) and keep in a warm room (for instance the airing cupboard).

After a few weeks the mealworms, fat and happy, will turn into creamy pupae, then into little black beetles, which

'Birds . . . have varying methods of hunting' (page 56)

represent your breeding stock. They lay eggs which hatch into mealworms, and so on. Crop the mealworms in accordance with all the scientific principles of MSY (maximum sustainable yield). If you want to start an empire, prepare other tins and prime them with a few bits of dry bread from an existing colony. These will carry beetle eggs.

After some weeks the mealworm city will be reduced to a dry powder, when you need to renew the vegetable layers and bran. You may also find it useful to feed your worms with a slice of damp bread every week. Fold a sheet of paper into a concertina and place this on top of the mix; this will serve as a resting place for mealworms and simplify collection.

Serve the mealworms in a fairly deep, round dish, so that they cannot escape – they are surprisingly mobile. Gentles are sometimes recommended but, though I have not tasted them myself and the birds certainly like them, they are less wholesome to handle than mealworms. (Gentles are fly maggots, whereas mealworms are the larval form of the beetle *Tenebrio molitor*.)

Ants' eggs (ant pupae) can be collected from under stones in your garden; it is rather hard work for small return but the birds will be grateful. And always put the stone back in place so as not to upset the other creatures whose roof it is.

Birds not only have varying food requirements, both in nature and at the bird table, but they also have varying methods of hunting. Some skulk about on the ground, some snoop along branches and foliage, and some run about on tree trunks and stone walls. So we must have variety of presentation as well as variety of food.

Bird tables

The traditional way of feeding is with a bird table and, although it has limitations, it is on the whole a very satisfactory method. The table can either be supported on a post or it can hang from the bough of a tree, or a bracket. Your own situation will probably decide the method you use. There is little to choose between the two systems so long as you keep the cat problem firmly in mind and do not fix the hanging model to a potential cat-way. The feeding tray should not be too small. Somewhere between the 2–4sq ft (30–60cm)

The simplest bird tables
are best . . .

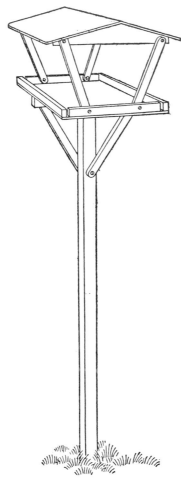

mark is ideal. Put a coaming round the edge to stop the food being blown off, but leave a gap in it somewhere so that the table can be cleared and cleaned easily, and water can run off.

Scrub the table with hot water and detergent, rinsing with cold water, in the autumn, so that it is germ-free for the winter feeding season.

Whether it hangs or stands on a pedestal or post, the tray should be about 5–6ft (1.5–1.8m) off the ground. The safest post is a piece of galvanised iron tubing, but any smooth pole will do, as long as you get it firmly into the ground. The most unsuitable support is one of those awful 'rustic' things that positively invite squirrels and cats to climb up to their burglarious work. The table should be in a position where it gets neither too much sun nor too much cold wind. It should be within reasonable distance – say, a couple of yards – of cover, but out of cat-jumping range. The point is that the woodland species, like blue tits, which frequent gardens, are not keen on a long flight over open ground to get to the table. Showing themselves too freely in the open makes them vulnerable to predators. Arrange things so that they can reach the haven of your bird table by way of short spurts between bushes, or sheds, or staging posts of some kind. If the terrain is open, provide hazel sticks at regular intervals. You'll soon learn the birds' requirements, and see how they like to survey a situation before exposing themselves.

The bird table does not need a roof but it is an advantage. A roof keeps the food drier, provides a place for a hanging seed-hopper, and may even be used as a roosting place at night. Birds will often use a covered bird table to shelter from a shower of rain. If the table has a roof-hopper, this should be kept full of mixed seed for the finches. On the tray, you can distribute your main offering of scraps and bird-pudding. Ideally, the food should be in pieces either so big that birds cannot carry it away, or so small that they do not want to carry it away: medium-sized bits tend to find their way to the nearest bush, where they get lost and encourage rats and mice. Another solution to this problem is to make a removable, close mesh, wire-netting frame which fits inside the coaming, covers the food, and prevents big birds flying off with large lumps. Arrange a couple of substantial twigs in such a way

. . . don't make access too easy for predators

67

that they provide 'queuing-space' for birds waiting their opportunity while a dominant individual is monopolising the tray.

Perhaps the most unusual of all bird tables is that provided by the Royal Navy. The RN Birdwatching Society has a 'Feed the Birds' campaign in which three vessels are experimenting with different feeds, provided for land birds on migration and far from home. These birds very often get relief from their exhaustion by resting on ships at sea. For instance, two female kestrels were fed with raw steak, and a racing pigeon did well on sweetcorn and peanuts. High in arctic latitudes, a brambling and two snow buntings were successfully fed on 'Swoop', and continued their journeys.

In hard winters snow buntings often penetrate as far south as Britain, and recently some of these exciting birds have been patronising a ground feeding station at the Aviemore Ski Centre in the Cairngorms. So keep your eyes open as you swish down the slopes.

Scrap baskets

The advantage of scrap baskets is that the food is less likely to get blown about and scattered. The disadvantage is that thrushes and blackbirds cannot manage to hang on to them when they are suspended. The simplest scrap container is one of those netting bags that comes with oranges or carrots at the greengrocer's. However, it will soon get rather messy and, in the long run, it is best to buy a wire basket specially made for the job.

Scrap baskets made of collapsible wire mesh must be avoided as, with these, there is a danger that small birds may get a foot jammed between two moving pieces of wire. Sharp edges and potential leg-damagers must, in fact, be watched for on all feeding devices. Many small birds get leg injuries, and it may be that ill-made bird feeders are often to blame. One unusual hazard with small scrap baskets is that they may be stolen by crows. All the crow family are enthusiastic collectors, and I well remember a rook once stealing a bar of soap from my camp site. If you find your scrap basket being borrowed in this way, fix the replacement more securely!

Seedhoppers

The only practical way of providing seed is from a hopper. All other methods are very wasteful. (Even the hopper is susceptible to the aggressive methods of jays and great tits, which scatter mixed seed while searching for titbits.) It is important to keep the seed dry and the hopper must have a good roof. The RSPB supply one which fits neatly into the roof of their standard bird table, but in a strong wind the seeds blow away much too wastefully. Their globe dispenser is far superior. (See page 80 for more information.) If you have been on autumn collecting expeditions, you will have a stock of your own seeds; if not, any pet shop will supply you with mixed wild bird seed or canary seed. Keep the hopper well filled, and do not risk a supply-failure in bad weather, because the finches will have become dependent on your generosity.

Nuts

Peanuts are a bird's best friend except in the breeding season, and the best way to present them is to have a special wire-netting box, preferably with a solid roof to keep the shelled nuts dry. (The RSPB and other bird furniture suppliers make excellent peanut feeders.) You may find yourself buying 3lb of nuts a week, but it will be in a good cause. If you hang whole peanuts, do not use multi-thread cotton or tits may get their legs trapped between the strands. The best plan is to take a thin piece of galvanized wire, about 18in (46cm) long, and cut it obliquely at one end to make a sharp point on which to skewer the nuts. Bend the top end into a hanging hook, and the bottom end slightly up to prevent the peanuts sliding off. Attach the wire to its anchor point by an elastic band, and the whole thing will twist around as birds perch on it. Tits particularly seem to enjoy twirling round in circles and are very amusing to watch. The peanut skewer can hang from the bird table or from a bough. Do not buy any of the feeders which are made of spiral wire which terminates in a point at the lower end. These are great leg-traps and should be avoided at all costs. (See pages 79–80 for various nut-feeders which can be safely recommended.) The important thing is that any feeder should lack 'bounciness' and avoid pinching legs. Tits and finches are the main customers for nuts in hanging devices, but unlikely species such as robins, dun-nocks, blackcaps and reed buntings, even pigeons, may solve the puzzle, to say nothing of squirrels.

Some Americans recommend clamping a jar of peanut butter to a bird table, and though I have not tried this myself, it should be worth experiment. But don't offer the stuff too freely, for it is a bit too sticky, and may clamp a bird's mandibles together. Mix equal parts of cornmeal with the peanut butter. You can prevent rain from getting in by fixing the jar at a slight downhill angle. For other uses of nuts you might like to try jamming brazils into odd cracks and crannies in trees; nuthatches will appreciate this sort of treasure hunt. Any chestnuts you have collected in the autumn can be boiled and crushed for the tits. Hazel nuts, acorns and beech-mast should be grated or chopped.

Bird-bell

It was the naturalist H. Mortimer Batten who made the tit-bell famous in the early days of *Children's Hour* on radio, and for many years his wooden design was made available to garden bird enthusiasts. Sadly it is no longer produced, but Robert Gillmor and I have persuaded the Dartmouth Pottery to make a glazed version which does the job quite well (see page 81). In essence it is a very simple device, making it possible to use up kitchen scraps in a way that allows only the most agile birds to get them, with a certain amount of difficulty. Thus the 'greedy' starlings and sparrows are held at arm's length. The pottery bell is turned upside down and placed in a mug or bowl and thus held firmly. It is primed with scraps and seeds, has a perch twig set in it, and is then filled with hot fat (not the sort which stays liquid at room temperature, though). See page 77 for recipe. When the mixture has set, you hang the bell up for tits, nuthatches and woodpeckers to explore. One of the advantages of the bird-bell is that it lasts a long time between replenishments, so it keeps your birds happy if you have to go away. Even the ground feeders get some benefit, when small pieces get dislodged and fall down. The advantage of the glazed bell is that it is easy to clean, but the RSPB have now produced an attractive version in terracotta which is perhaps more 'natural'. If you do not wish to buy a bird-bell you can make a perfectly good substitute from a half-coconut, the original and cheapest version!

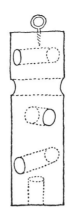

Another useful hanging device is the suet stick. For this, bore 1in holes through a short length of birch log, stuff the holes with raw beef or kidney suet and hang it up. Woodpeckers are very fond of this gadget, but avoid fancy perches, or the starlings will take over (see drawing, above).

Ground feeding stations

Many birds are reluctant to come to the bird table. Blackbirds and thrushes, dunnock and even moorhens will all prefer to feed on the ground. The best plan is to put down a special tray for them, so that it can be taken in at night. Otherwise you will be encouraging rats. Do not put the tray too near a possible cat hiding-place, but see that it is within about 6ft (1.8m) or so of cover. Just outside my window, as I write, there are three dunnocks, a pair of yellowhammers, a chaffinch and a greenfinch all feeding happily on the ground below the bird table. Great tits get into the bird table seed-hopper and scatter the seeds as they search for bits of walnut, so that there are always easy pickings on the ground below. Many birds will hunt for crumbs under a bird table, and you may prefer to provide these groundfeeders with a nut-hopper of their own. If you are plagued with sparrows, a coarse wheat hopper, placed well away from your more expensive seed devices, may keep them occupied.

Not all of the seeds which fall to the ground will be found and eaten by birds. Some may lie there and, in time, germinate. And your bird table may sprout in due course from a truly

The feeding tray should not be too small - around three or four square feet is ideal. A coaming stops food blowing off.

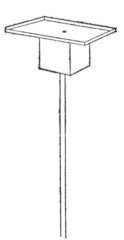

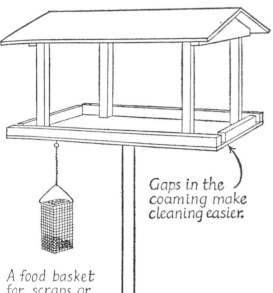

The R.S.P.B. table (above) is complete with chains for hanging and an adaptor for fitting to a post.

A food hopper is shown fitted under the roof.

Gaps in the coaming make cleaning easier.

A food basket for scraps or nuts is very popular with tits.

A galvanised tube or smooth pole is ideal.

About five or six feet high.

A biscuit tin fixed under the table is a useful anti-squirrel device.

exotic garden of unexpected plants. David McClintock, the distinguished botanist, carried out some fascinating experiments in which, instead of offering commercial bird food to the birds, he planted it. He was puzzled by the strange names which were given by the seedsmen, and found, after much research, that seeds called 'Blue Maw' and 'Dari', which are not found in botanical books, revealed themselves as opium poppy *Papaver somniferum* and the annual tropical cereal *Sorghum bicolor* when they were encouraged to grow and reveal themselves as plants.

For the enthusiast, I reproduce the table which crowned his efforts, first published in the periodical *New Scientist*.

Aniseed	*Pimpinella anisum*
Blue maw	*Papaver somniferum*
Buckwheat	*Fagopyrum esculentum*
Mazagan canary	*Phalaris canariensis*
Chicory	*Cichorium intybus*
Dari	*Sorghum bicolor*
Gold of pleasure	*Camelina sativa*
Hemp	*Cannabis sativa*
White kardi	*Carthamnus tinctorius*
White lettuce	*Lactuca sativa*
Best Dutch linseed	*Linum usitassimum*
Chinese millet	*Setaria italica*
Japanese millet	*Echinochloa utilis*
Plate yellow millet	*Panicum miliaceum*
White millet	*Panicum miliaceum*
Niger	*Guizotia abyssinica*
Panicum millet	*Setaria italica*
Black rape	*Brassica campestris*
German rübsen	*Brassica campestris*
Chinese safflower	*Carthamnus tinctorius*
Striped sunflower seed	*Helianthus annuus*
French teazle	*Dipsacus sativus*

Window-sills

Even if you do not have a garden, you can still have a lot of fun providing a specialised bird-feeding station at your window-sill. You might devise a special adaptor for clamping the bird table to a sill, and most of the hanging devices can easily be suspended from a bracket. And even if you have a splendid garden, a window-sill feeding station is still desirable because, as sparrows and starlings are shy of it, you will be able to put out special delicacies for special birds. If possible, use a window-sill that is reasonably sheltered from both hot sun and cold winds. And, whatever feeding arrangements you may have, always remember that a constant supply of water is absolutely essential.

Selection problems

Some people have a most unreasonable hatred of starlings. Personally, I find them beautiful and amusing to watch, although they can, occasionally, rather overwhelm one's facilities by sheer weight of numbers. By almost every post in the winter I get letters from people asking how they can make sure that other birds besides starlings get their fair share of the food. Sparrows, too, can be a nuisance as they tend to dominate other birds. The problem is that both starlings and sparrows are omnivorous and show a healthy interest in almost any food that is offered, so they are extra difficult to select against.

One way to cheat the starlings is to feed early or late. Starlings are late risers, and as they also flock away to roost early in the afternoon, you can cheat them with early morning and evening feeds for your garden residents. Another trick is to make a feeding cage of wire-mesh netting with an aperture too narrow for starlings to penetrate. If you put $1\frac{1}{8}$in (29mm) welded mesh netting round your bird table, it should keep the starlings out. The only disadvantage is that it also keeps thrushes and blackbirds out.

Starlings and sparrows tend to be shyer than other birds, so if you provide a feeding patch for them well away from your house and bird table, they may patronise it in preference to the 'home' feeding stations. This is where a window-sill comes into its own, providing tits, robins and finches with a reward for their tameness. I have already mentioned that a wheat-hopper may keep your sparrows busy while you feed tasty morsels to your favourites.

But do try to develop a more friendly attitude towards starlings. One of their problems, from a bird-gardener's point of view, is that there are so many of them, and it is odd to realise that only a hundred years or so ago they were quite rare in some parts of the country. One of my correspondents, Mrs Dorothy Coomber of Bridlington in Yorkshire, had a starling which was part of the wild household for fourteen years. Recognisable because of a deformed foot, it soon became tame and was fed regularly. For many years she had brought her fledglings to be fed and, when Mrs Coomber moved to another house a short distance away, the starling followed suit! The bird's favourite food is cheese, and it has to be *Cheshire* cheese; no other is acceptable.

If you can feed at the same time every day, it is far and away the best method. Animals have built-in clocks and appreciate regularity. Early morning is best of all, as birds lose weight overnight and need a good start to the day. Obviously, the most important season for feeding is winter, when natural food supplies are scarce, and during a hard spell you may hold the lives of many small birds in your hands. So once again, I must emphasise that once you start feeding you must not stop, until the warm days of spring. It is far better not to put out scraps at all if it is likely that, having started, you may later have to stop. The birds soon become dependent on your daily supplies, and if they are not forthcoming during cold weather when the ground is hard with frost, many of your customers die. It is true that they have feathers which insulate them from the cold, but a body cannot function and keep warm without fuel.

At the beginning of April, gradually reduce the amount of food you put out. The pattern of feeding should be altered. The amounts of heating foods such as suet and hemp should be severely reduced, and less bread should be given as this may fill a nestling bird with low-value bulk. Stale cake is better than peanuts for nestlings, but live insect food is best of all, and this is what the parents supply. At this time of year it is arguably best not to feed at all, since most garden birds alter their feeding habits to take advantage of the abundance of insect food. Put out some mealworms and ant pupae, if you wish, though this is the season when the birds are repaying you for your winter largesse. They will destroy hordes of insect pests far more safely than any chemical pesticide.

If you feed throughout the spring, summer and autumn, use very much smaller quantities. This will keep your birds tame and, when you start increasing their supplies in late autumn, your happy band of pensioners will already know the ropes.

Birds which visit feeding stations . . .

Blackbird	Moorhen
Blackcap	Partridge, Grey
Brambling	Partridge, Red-legged
Bullfinch	Pheasant
Bunting, Cirl	Pigeon, Wood
Bunting, Corn	Pigeon, Rock
Bunting, Reed	Rail, Water
Bunting, Snow	Redpoll, Lesser
Chaffinch	Redwing
Chiffchaff	Robin
Crossbill	Rook
Dipper	Siskin
Dove, Collared	Sparrow, House
Dove, Rock	Sparrow, Tree
Dunnock	Sparrowhawk
Fieldfare	Starling
Firecrest	Swan, Mute
Goldcrest	Thrush, Mistle
Goldfinch	Thrush, Song
Goose, Canada	Tit, Bearded
Goose, Pink-footed	Tit, Blue
Goshawk	Tit, Coal
Greenfinch	Tit, Great
Gull, Black-headed	Tit, Marsh
Gull, Herring	Tit, Long-tailed
Hawfinch	Tit, Willow
Heron, Grey	Treecreeper
Jackdaw	Turnstone
Jay	Wagtail, Pied
Kestrel	Wheatear
Kingfisher	Woodpecker, Great Spotted
Linnet	Woodpecker, Green
Magpie	Woodpecker, Lesser Spotted
Mallard	Wren
Merlin	Yellowhammer

Recipes from the Bird Table School of Cookery

BASIC PUD

Take seeds, peanuts, cheese, oatmeal, dry cake and scraps. Put them in a container, pour hot fat over the mixture until it is covered, and leave to set. Turn out onto a table, unless you have prepared it in a tit-bell or coconut holder. Rough quantities: 1lb (400g) of mixture to ½lb (200g) of melted fat.

TIT-BELL RECIPE

Fill the upturned bell with seeds, peanuts, cheese, oatmeal, sultanas, cake crumbs and other scraps. Pour in hot fat to the brim. Insert a short piece of twig into the mix to act as a learner's perch, if necessary. Leave to harden. Turn the bell over and hang in a suitable place where small birds like blue tits are already accustomed to come for food.

EDWIN COHEN'S PUDDING

Mix 8oz (200g) melted beef suet, 12oz (300g) coarse oatmeal and 2–3oz (50–75g) flour with 5oz (125g) water to stiff paste. Bake in shallow pie dish to form flat cake at 175°C (350°F, Gas Mark 4) for approximately one hour.

MISS TURNER'S MAIZE CAKE

Mix 3oz (75g) maize meal in a bowl with equal quantities of chopped nuts, hemp, canary and millet seed. Stir with boiling water till coagulated, and add two beaten eggs. Tie tightly in a cloth and bake at 175°C (350°F, Gas Mark 4) for fifty minutes to one hour.

TIM'S BIRD CAKE

Mix 2lb (1kg) self-raising flour, 8oz (200g) margarine and a little sugar with water and bake like a rock bun.

MAX KNIGHT MIX

Mix stale cake and fat with a few dried currants and sultanas. Imprisoned in a 5–8in (12.5–20cm) wire-mesh bag, it keeps birds busy and prevents too much scatter.

ANTI-SPARROW PUDDING

Boil together one cup of sugar and one cup of water for five minutes. Mix with one cup of melted fat (suet, bacon or ordinary shortening) and leave it to cool. Then mix with breadcrumbs, flour, bird seed, a little boiled rice and scraps, until the mixture is very stiff. Pack into any kind of tin can or glass jar. Lay the can on its side in a tree, on the window sill, or any place where birds can perch and pick out the food. The can must be placed securely so that the birds cannot dislodge it, nor rain get inside. May not fool sparrows for long, though, so don't take it too seriously.

Feeding regime

It is in the winter that your bird table offerings make maximum impact, because that is the season when wild food is least abundant. In spite of the recipes, the fact is that almost any food or food mix will be sampled by one bird or another, but remember to avoid mouldy or salted peanuts. And once you have started to offer food, continue on a regular basis, putting it out at the same time every day if possible.

Gradually reduce the offerings as the days lengthen in spring and natural food becomes more freely available, but continue to provide seeds for your finches until the end of April.

Suppliers of bird food

E. W. Coombs Ltd, 25 Frindsbury Road, Strood, Kent. Sluis Universal Bird Food; mealworms; seed mixture.

John E. Haith Ltd, Park Street, Cleethorpes, Lincolnshire. Haith's Wild Bird Food; softbill food, tit food (in bulk); peanut kernels and shells; sunflower seeds (mixed).

Wholefood Ltd, 112 Baker Street, London W1. Wheat, rye, oats, barley, rice, buckwheat and millet, whole grain grown organically without the use of chemical pesticides.

Suppliers of bird furniture

Royal Society for the Protection of Birds, The Lodge, Sandy, Bedfordshire SG19 2DL. Free catalogue on application. All the RSPB equipment is made of high-quality weather-resistant materials. The woodwork is treated with a harmless preservative and painting is unnecessary. Instructions and advice are included where necessary.

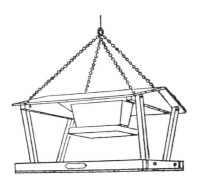

RSPB BIRD TABLE, illustrated above, is 18in × 12in (45cm × 30cm), well proportioned. It may be suspended by chains or fixed on to a 4sq in (10cm × 10cm) post. Chains and post socket supplied as standard fitments, but *not* the post. The roof overlaps the table slightly and ensures that food is kept dry in most conditions, although strong winds and driving rain inevitably play havoc. But this is the best buy in bird tables. The roof is fitted with rails to take a food-hopper, which slides into place well sheltered.

HANGING BRACKET, for suspending the table, from a tree, wall

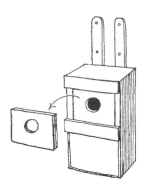

or window frame. Strong and rust-resistant.

SEED HOPPER, for dispensing seed mixtures. Fits neatly under bird table roof, for which it is specially made. Hoppers can be very tiresome gadgets, as they are so susceptible to wind and to rain-jamming. Spherical version, see page 80, is better.

DRINKING TRAY, made in fibreglass with simulated stone finish to harmonise with rockery, or to disguise an unsightly manhole cover. 20in × 15in (50cm × 38cm).

STANDARD NESTBOX, for hole-nesting species with 1⅛in (29mm) diameter entrance hole to exclude sparrows. Removable top for cleaning. Highly recommended. Illustrated above.

Metal entrance-hole protector, which prevents squirrels, woodpeckers, etc, enlarging the hole.

OPEN-FRONT NESTBOX for robins, spotted flycatchers, etc.

SPIRAL TIT FEEDER, with window bracket and suction cup.

TIT FEEDER, more substantial affair, wooden box with wire mesh access to peanuts. 6in × 3½in (15cm × 8.8cm).

FOOD BASKET, a strong, wire mesh basket, plastic-coated for rust prevention, with lid, to take shelled peanuts or scraps, 5½in × 3in (13.8cm × 7.5cm). Illustrated on left.

DINABIRD FEEDER, good for offering 'Swoop'. 13in (32.5cm) acrylic tube dispenses seed and peanuts through six feeding ports.

SPHERICAL SEED FEEDER, weatherproof plastic sphere, 7in (17.5cm) diameter.

WINDOW FEEDER, acrylic design, suction pads attach it to your window. Ideal for flat-dwellers.

TERRACOTTA TIT-BELL, with seed in attractive gift box. And many other devices . . . send for catalogue.

Nerine Nurseries, Welland, Malvern, Worcestershire WR13 6LN. Bird tables, tit boxes, robin boxes and the useful house martin nests. These act as a magnet to this species and encourage the establishment of a colony. The nests are fixed under the eaves of house or barn. Sometimes house sparrows may worm their way in by enlarging the holes but Nerine Nurseries supply a leaflet with instructions for a simple anti-

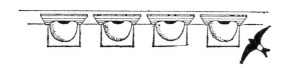

sparrow method. Incidentally this method, involving a screen of 12in (30cm) weighted cords, 2½in (63mm) apart, and hung 6in (15cm) away from the entrance hole, can be used to protect natural house martin nests as well.

Pippaware, 122 Ennerdale Road, Richmond-upon-Thames, TW9 2DH. Wild bird feeding table and 'Happy Bird' nest box.

Scandinavian Design, 13 Hillside Road, Marlow, Buckinghamshire SL7 3JU. Glass-sided nestbox, bird tables, feeders, etc. Send for brochure 'garden bird equipment'.

Jamie Wood Ltd, Cross Street, Polegate, Sussex. Suppliers of bird furniture, hides, etc. SAE for brochure.

Scottish National Institution for the War Blinded, Linburn, Wilkieston, by Kirknewton, Midlothian. Wire and wood feeding devices, nestboxes, bird tables and tit-bells. Send for illustrated leaflet.

Sutton Parva Nurseries, Heytesbury, Wiltshire. Dutch nesting baskets for duck.

National Trust Shop, Killerton, Broadclyst, Devon EX5 3LE, for the glazed pottery bird-bell in smart box.

Warning. Avoid any peanut feeder which involves a flexible coiled-spring system. These are highly dangerous, since a bird may get its feet jammed when another flies away from the feeder causing the spring to contract. And avoid all-in-one nestbox/feeding-tray/water-trough devices. It is asking for trouble to invite birds to eat or drink at the doorstep to another bird's house, creating territorial stresses and strains which don't do anyone any good!

5 Predators and poisons

A bird's life is fraught with natural hazards. After surviving a cold winter, it may get snapped up by a sparrowhawk. If it succeeds in finding a mate and hatching young, there may be a sudden shortage of food and the weaker nestlings may die. The chances of a wild bird living to a ripe old age are so remote as to be almost non-existent. So if we are going to invite birds to join us in our gardens there is an obligation on us to try to reduce the hazards, while recognising the fact that the predator-prey relationship is basically a healthy one, with advantage for both parties.

Ideally, of course, you should completely seal your garden from unwelcome predators, but this is more easily said than done. Sparrowhawks and weasels are all part of the natural scene (weasels are adept at raiding nestboxes), but domestic cats and grey squirrels are less acceptable. Ideally, there is no place for them in the bird garden, but you will never keep them out, short of total war. If you have a cat of your own, at least it serves the useful purpose of discouraging alien cats in defending its territory. And you might like to consider keeping it in for a reasonable and regular period each morning and before dusk, in order to give the birds time to feed. I have to admit that I like the company of a cat and would not care to be without one, but the fact remains that Great Britain is home to many millions of cats, every one of them superfluous to a good bird garden. You must make your own decisions, but one thing is certain. You should not try to *tame* your garden birds if you keep a cat. Feed them and make homes for them by all means, but don't encourage them to become too friendly or there will, inevitably, be a tragic outcome.

If you don't want to go as far as installing a wire fence, the best substitute is a thick and prickly hedge. Hawthorn or holly hedges will both in time become fairly impenetrable, although you will always have to watch for secret passageways and block them with bramble or thorn cuttings. The disadvantage of a clipped hedge is that it will not fruit very freely, though, on the other hand, it provides good nesting sites. Allow some of the plants to mature so that a few trees grow out of the hedge to blossom and fruit. Holly is particularly good, because the dead leaves cover the soil underneath with spiny points which may deter cats, weasels and such like.

Rats have to be taken seriously. They climb well, even shinning up trees and hedges to search for eggs and young birds, and a good bird garden is also an attractive rat garden. So food should not be left on the ground at night, and windfalls too should be cleared away every evening: they can become part of the winter bird table menu.

The best way to deal with rats is to use a safe poison, or to put plenty of traps under cover in the dark places they like. Place a 5–6ft (1.5–1.8m) drainpipe (6in (15cm) section) in the likely places, and put a killer food bait – 'Raticate' or 'Warfarin' are probably the safest – in the middle of it. Mechanical rat-traps are only moderately successful. Rats are suspicious creatures and if you try traps put one each side of a bait placed in the middle of the pipe-length. Cheese, apple, cake, almost anything will do as bait. Set the traps before dusk and examine them when it is dark. Don't leave them set up all night or you might trap a cat.

Grey squirrels, too, are unwelcome visitors to the bird garden. They may appear charmingly acrobatic as they leap from branch to branch, but they are great egg-eaters. They will even enlarge the hole of a nestbox to lift out the nestlings. You must harden your heart and shoot or trap them. You might want to discourage jays and magpies, for there is no doubt that they will take any small birds' eggs and young they can find. On the other hand, they are handsome birds in their own right.

The greatest bird menace of all is the organochlorine insecticide. After years of trial and a growing weight of evidence against them, it is depressing to find that farmers still use dangerous seed-dressings and sprays, and that garden shops still sell harmful and extravagant garden 'aids'. If you have the least feeling for wildlife and, incidentally, if you value your own health, you should refuse to use organo-chlorine pesticides and you should encourage others to do the same. Our environment is becoming increasingly pol-luted with chemicals whose long term effects are unknown but highly suspect. Many of the pesticides sold freely in shops are dangerous, not only to the pests they set out to destroy but to useful animals, as well as, ultimately, to ourselves.

Nowadays, unlike the sad days of 1960 and '61 when enormous numbers of birds died as a result of ignorant use of toxic chemicals, the situation has improved. The sight of birds falling from the sky or writhing in agony has become quite rare, but the present relatively encouraging position with regard to birds of prey is not comfortable enough for any complacency. There is not much doubt that many farmers stockpiled dangerous chemicals such as Aldrin and Dieldrin before the ban was introduced; and dangerous sheep-dips and seed-dressings are still being used. Only a few heavily contaminated prey are needed to kill a hawk, falcon or owl. And even if the bird is not killed, its fertility may be affected.

I do not suggest that we stop waging war against garden pests, but it is worth pointing out that sprays do dangerously just that which birds do safely. Finches, tits, treecreepers and wrens all patrol and police leafy places and control the caterpillar and insect population. Thrushes (and hedgehogs) help with your snails and slugs. Encourage the birds, save yourself money, and give yourself pleasure at the same time. It is true that birds will also eat some of your soft fruit and spoil some of the buds of your fruit trees, but this is a small price to pay for the pleasure they will give and for the knowledge that yours is a poison-free garden. On balance, birds do more good than harm.

As a gardener with a commitment to the principles of conservation, you will naturally want to use chemicals sparingly in protecting your plants from pests with the least harm to wildlife. The RSPB has prepared these lists which may be helpful in choosing pesticides which cause least damage.

There are a large number of pesticides for garden use on the market and the chemicals recommended by the RSPB are the active ingredients of products that are sold under a variety of proprietary brand names. After deciding that you really need to use one of them, check the manufacturer's label carefully to make sure that the product contains the right chemical for the job. The Government's Pesticides Safety Precautions Scheme assesses the hazards which any new chemical or formulations may present to wildlife and also lays down precautions that should be taken for the safe use of the chemical.

Safety
All chemicals should be used with great care. Here are two points to consider before buying them:
1 Only use a pesticide if you can identify what is affecting your plants – it may not be a pest.
2 Pesticides may affect harmless species as well as the pests they are intended for.
If you must use a pesticide then remember that you are using a poisonous substance and take the following precautions.
Always
● Obey the manufacturer's instructions.
● Wash hands and utensils carefully after use.
● Keep chemicals out of reach of children and pets.
● Avoid contaminating bird baths, water tanks and particularly ponds, streams and ditches – fish are susceptible to many chemicals, even when they are diluted.
● Avoid spraying plants when they are in flower, to reduce

the risks to bees and other pollinating or nectar-feeding insects. If you must spray at this stage, then do so in the evening. Do not spray when there is a risk of the chemical drifting in the wind. This is particularly important when applying herbicides as a fine mist spray can severely affect herbaceous plants.

● Only buy the quantity of chemical that you need.

● Unwanted liquids should be well diluted and emptied into an outside drain, WC or onto bare soil. Solid products should be sealed into the container and placed in a dustbin. Used containers should be rinsed out before putting them in the dustbin. Any special disposal instructions will be marked on the label. Aerosol containers must not be placed on or near a fire as they can be explosive.

Herbicides (Weedkillers)

Although most herbicides are not directly harmful to animals and birds, care should be taken when spraying, especially where gardens adjoin hedgerows. Remember that seeds and fruits of weeds like dandelions, docks, groundsel, nettles and thistles provide food for finches, so do not get rid of them unless you have to. The following products are preferred, but make sure that the one you buy is suitable for the plants you are treating.

Specific uses	*Recommended treatment*
Established lawns:	
Clovers	Mecoprop with 2, 4-D, dicamba or ioxynil.
Daisy	2, 4-D with mecoprop or dicamba.
Dandelion, creeping buttercup and plantains	MCPA, 2, 4-D or 2, 4-D mixtures.
Moss	Lawn sand based on ferrous compounds.
Variety of weeds	MCPA with dicamba or 2, 4-D with dicamba or mecoprop.
Newly laid lawns:	No herbicides for at least six months.
Paths, drives and tennis courts:	Simazine or paraquat granules.
Vegetable gardens and flower beds:	
Clearing weeds before planting	Glyphosate.

Specific uses	Recommended treatment
Removing annual weeds from ornamentals, strawberries and certain vegetables	Propachlor granules.
Problem weeds:	
Couch grass	Dalapon, used when grass is growing vigorously, but among fruit trees and bushes, apply in November when tree is dormant. Glyphosate can also be used.
Bindweed, coltsfoot, dock and horsetail	MCPA, 2, 4-D or 2, 4-D mixtures.
Dandelion	2, 4-D or 2, 4-D mixtures.
Ground elder	Dichlobenil, when desirable plants cannot be damaged.
Nettles	MCPA, 2, 4-D or mecoprop.

Rodent control
For indoor control, when mice are attacking stored bulbs or fruit, a break-back trap may be used. These should not be used for outdoor control. When mice and voles are eating plants, rodenticides may be used. Warfarin is a poison and should be placed in a pipe where only rodents can find it.

Bird deterrents
Anthraquinone is sold to protect buds from attack from birds and is relatively non-toxic. Ammonium aluminium sulphate is used as a repellant on vegetables and flowers. The effectiveness of these two products varies depending upon conditions.

Earthworms
Although worm casts may be unsightly, worms are beneficial in providing aeration and improving soil drainage.

Insecticides
Take care that beneficial insects such as bees and ladybirds are not harmed when insecticides are being used. Some chemicals have adverse effects on particular plants and you must make sure that the product you are using is suitable.

Specific uses	Recommended treatment
Ants	Permethrin, pyrethrum.
Aphids – on fruits	Spray before blossoming with dimethoate, formothion, malathion or chlorpyrifos.
– on vegetables and ornamental plants	Fenitrothion, malathion or pirimicarb. (Some plants can be damaged by these – check before use.)
Caterpillars on vegetables	Chlorpyrifos, derris or permethrin.
Cabbage fly	Bromophos or chlorpyrifos.
Carrot fly	Bromophos or chlorpyrifos.
Codling moth	Chlorpyrifos, permethrin or fenitrothion.
Cutworms	Bromophos or chlorpyrifos.
Onion fly	Bromophos or chlorpyrifos.
Raspberry beetle	Derris dust, fenitrothion or malathion.
Red spider mite	Derris (roses), dimethoate, malathion or chlorpyrifos.
Sawflies	Chlorpyrifos, dimethoate or fenitrothion.
Thrips	Derris (roses), fenitrothion or malathion.
Wasps	Carbaryl.
Winter moths on fruit trees	Chlorpyrifos, fenitrothion or permethrin.

Slug control

The two main ingredients of slug killers are metaldehyde and methiocarb, both of which can be harmful to wildlife and pets if misused. The bait should not be sprinkled around, but should be covered with a brick, board or flowerpot to prevent non-target species such as birds and hedgehogs feeding on it, or on poisoned slugs.

A simple way to catch slugs is to sink a shallow, steep-sided container into the ground and fill it with a sweet liquid such as beer. Alternatively, a hollowed-out half orange or grapefruit placed open face down will attract them.

Timber preservation and bats

Bats are killed by organochlorine and organophosphorus compounds which are used for the treatment of roof timbers. If you wish to treat roof timbers without harming them, contact Dr R. Stebbings, Monks Wood Experimental Research Station, Abbots Ripton, Cambridgeshire PE17 2LS (Tel: Abbots Ripton 381).

Fungicides

Most fungicides are unlikely to harm animals and birds, but many harm fish. The following chemicals are preferable to mercury-based compounds such as calomel (mercurous chloride) which should not be used.

Specific uses	*Recommended treatment*
Blight on potato and tomato	Copper, maneb or zineb.
Bulb and corm diseases	Treat before planting with quintozene dust; dip in benomyl or thiophanate-methyl.
Damping-off of seedlings	Copper or quintozene; thiram (as seed dressing).
Leaf spots	Benomyl, copper, maneb (roses), thiophanate-methyl, thiram or zineb.
Mildews: Downy	Zineb
Powdery	Benomyl, copper, dinocap, sulphur, thiophanate-methyl
Moulds – on soft fruit	Benomyl, dichlofluanid, thiophanate-methyl or thiram.
– on vegetables and pot plants	As above. Under glass use tecnazine.
Rusts	Maneb, thiram or zineb.
Scabs on apples and pears	Benomyl, copper, sulphur (not sulphur-shy varieties), thiophanate-methyl or thiram.
Turf diseases	Quintozene or thiophanate-methyl.

Further information on the uses of individual chemical products can be found in the 'List of Approved Products and their Uses for Farmers and Growers', which is revised each year and should be available from your local library.

References

British Agrochemicals Association, *Directory of Garden Chemicals* (1981) B.A.A.
British Crop Protection Council, *The Pesticide Manual* (1979) B.C.P.C.

MAFF, *List of Approved Products and their Uses for Farmers and Growers* (1981) HMSO.

Fryer, D. & Makepeace, R. J., *Weed Control Handbook*, Vol II (1978) Blackwell.

Martin, H. & Worthing, C. R., *Insecticide and Fungicide Handbook for Crop Protection* (1977) Blackwell.

Buczacki, S., Harris, K. & Hargreaves, B., *Collins Guide to the Pests, Diseases and Disorders of Garden Plants* (1981) Collins.

To save yourself needless expense and to develop a healthy poison-free garden, get a copy of an invaluable booklet *Pest Control Without Poisons*, by Lawrence D. Hills, published by the Henry Doubleday Research Association, Bocking, Braintree, Essex. Write to them for a copy of their list of 'safe' pesticides.

And please don't ask me to define what is and what is not a pest, because I have the uncomfortable feeling that you and I might be prime candidates. Live and let live.

6   Species notes

These notes provide basic information about those birds
which patronise artificially-provided nest places. Status and
distribution, habitat, food and feeding, nest and nesting is
summarised. There is no information on identification, since
this would run away with too much space and I am assuming
that a field guide is essential to any bird gardener's library.

One of the best reference books for bird identification is *A
Field Guide to the Birds of Britain and Europe,* by Peterson,
Mountfort and Hollom, published by Collins. For identification notes plus detailed information on habitat, distribution, behaviour, food and breeding (in the wild) the most
useful single volume is *The Popular Handbook of British
Birds,* by P. A. D. Hollom, published by H. F. and G.
Witherby. Further information on nestboxes can be found in
the pamphlet *Nestboxes,* published by the BTO (address page
168).

This list is assembled in the internationally accepted Voous
order of classification, its advantage lying in the fact that the
birds are arranged in a sequence of related families which
makes taxonomic sense. An alphabetical list is provided in

the general index at the back of this book.

NB 'Interior depth' refers to the distance from the bottom of the entrance hole to the floor of the box, *not* from floor to ceiling.

Additions and corrections to the food preference and nestbox sections in the following notes will be welcomed.

Diver, Red-throated *Gavia stellata*
Local in Scottish Highlands, islands, Orkney, Shetland and Donegal. Pools, lochs, marsh and moor. Outside breeding season is marine.
Fish, maybe molluscs and crustacea etc.
Nests close to water, within 1yd (9m) or so, usually on islets, sometimes at lochside. A mere scrape in the vegetation; sometimes a platform of vegetation.
Artificial nest site: In Argyll, where the divers were suffering from a good deal of disturbance both by fishermen and hydro-electric scheme water fluctuations, local enthusiasts found that the birds would accept a raft as a nest site. Empty plastic containers topped with heavy-gauge wire netting, planted with turves and bound with yet more wire netting, were anchored in suitable hill lochs.
Eggs: Usually 2 yellowish-olive to brown. Late May or June. Incubation 24–29 days, fledging about 8 weeks. One brood.

Diver, Black-throated *Gavia arctica*
Local in Scottish Highlands. Large lochs.
See Diver, red-throated.

Grebe, Great crested *Podiceps cristatus*
Breeds regularly in most English counties except Devon & Cornwall. Scarcer in Scotland and Wales. Lakes, reservoirs, gravel pits and large ponds with reedy cover.
Dives for fish, insects, tadpoles, etc.
Naturally nests among reeds or vegetation close to edge, made of water plants, reeds, perhaps twigs, just above surface.
Artificial nest site: May adopt the sort of raft put up by wildfowl enthusiasts for geese and ducks (see page 95).
Eggs: Usually 3–4 chalky white, become grained duration incubation. End March onwards. Incubation 28 days; fledging 9–10 weeks. Sometimes two broods.

Fulmar *Fulmarus glacialis*

Summer visitor, breeding on coastal cliffs more or less round the whole of the British Isles. Otherwise at sea in the North Atlantic.

Feeds on molluscs, fish, etc. Takes fish-offal thrown overboard from fishing vessels.

Nests on cliff slopes and ledges, on bare rock or soil. Sometimes the female makes a slight hollow.

Artificial nest site: Has taken to excavated ledges provided in Norfolk cliffs, along stretches where there are few natural sites. On exposed cliffs, where there are patches of sand in the boulder clay, dig out a ledge about 1ft (30cm) wide and 6in to 8in (15cm to 20cm) deep in the sand. The birds do the rest.

Eggs: White. Late May. Incubation 8 weeks; fledging 8 weeks. One brood.

Read: *The Fulmar* by James Fisher, Collins, 1952.

Heron, Grey *Ardea cinerea*

Resident throughout British Isles, wherever there is water not too deep for wading.

Mainly fish, but much else. Fish farmers objecting to heron visitors should contact the RSPB. May come to bird table for kitchen scraps, will come to garden pond for goldfish, etc.

Nests in tree canopies, colonially. Single nests sometimes found which may signal the founding of a new colony. Bulky structure of branches, sticks, lined with smaller twigs.

Artificial nest site: May take advantage of a platform on chicken wire frame firmly placed high in Scots pine or other suitable tree.

Eggs: 3–5 greenish-blue. February or March. Incubation about 25 days; fledging about 50–55 days. Sometimes two broods.

Read: *The Heron* by Frank A. Lowe, Collins, 1954.

Swan, Mute *Cygnus olor*

Generally distributed. Open water, ponds, parks, sheltered estuaries, sea coast and lochs.

Dips head and neck, or 'up-ends' to graze on underwater vegetation; also takes roots and buds of aquatic plants, small frogs, tadpoles, fish. Will come to hand or feeding station for scraps.

Nests anywhere near water, on large heap of vegetation.
Artificial nest site: Takes readily to a suitable raft, both on freshwater and on estuaries. Prime with a pile of vegetation.
Eggs: 5–7 almost white, tinged with greyish- or bluish-green. April or May. Incubation about 35 days; fledging about 4½ months. One brood. Warning: aggressive at nest.
Read: *The Royal Birds*, Lillian Grace Paca, St Martin's Press, New York, 1963; *The Swans*, Sir Peter Scott and The Wildfowl Trust, 1972; *The Mute Swan*, John Fair, Croom Helm, 1986.

Goose, Greylag   *Anser anser*

In summer, hilly heather moors, islands. Feral birds breed more freely by freshwater sites such as reservoirs, gravel pits and lakes, mainly in islands.
Food: grasses, cereals.
Nests on the ground. Heather or twigs, grasses, mosses, with down and feathers.
Artificial nest site: Has regularly nested on rafts in suitable locations.
Eggs: 4–6 creamy white. Last half of April. Incubation 27–28 days; fledging about 8 weeks. One brood.
Read: *Wild Geese*, M. A. Ogilvie, Poyser, 1978.

Goose, Canada   *Branta canadensis*

Was introduced to Britain as a status symbol, ornamenting stately lakes, in eighteenth century. Has since become a successful feral species, enjoying grassland and marshes by freshwater ponds and lakes.
Grazes in flocks on grassland. Also takes water plants. Will come to hand-feed on corn or bread when tame.
Nests on islands and marshes, sheltered by undergrowth or bush. Nest-hollow lined with grasses, leaves, reeds, down and feathers.
Artificial nest site: Box or platform raised on posts above water level or on raft. Make an artificial island, plant clumps of iris, reeds, sedge, etc to provide a nest site. Since the expansion of gravel pit workings of the last few decades they have taken advantage of the spoil islands which remain when the pits are worked out and flooded. In Canada, where they sometimes nest in suitable tree sites such as broken stumps or

in the hollows left by fallen branches, this propensity has been exploited by egg collectors. Wooden platforms, up to 65ft (20m) above ground, or on top of 10ft (3m) poles where there are no trees, are soon colonised. Try sawn-off barrels or open tubs, suitably drained, and offering a platform some 2ft (60cm) across and 1ft (30cm) deep.

Eggs: 5 or 6 white. Late March or April. Incubation 4 weeks; fledging 6 weeks. One brood. Warning: Canada geese (gander especially) can be very aggressive in the breeding season, and have been known to attack human beings, even wounding children.

Shelduck *Tadorna tadorna*
Generally distributed round low-lying coast and estuaries.
Food: marine molluscs, crustaceans, etc.
Nests in rabbit burrows, bramble tunnels, in gorse and bracken, sometimes in walls, hollow trees. Lined with down plus some vegetation.
Nestbox: Ideally on an island free from predators. Plastic pipe or old milk churn set in bank. May be persuaded to nest in a fruit box in a hollow in vegetation, for instance wild rose or bramble bushes surrounded by long grass or bracken. Or sink a small barrel into the ground, with just a 6in (15cm) entrance hole showing. Provide a 1ft (30cm) cube nest chamber approached by a length of 9in (23cm) drain pipe. Simulate a rabbit burrow. (May also be successful for Manx shearwaters, storm petrels and puffins, in suitable habitat.)

9"(23cm) diameter drainpipe

12"(30cm) cube timber nest chamber

A shelduck nest tunnel

Eggs: 8–15 creamy-white. May. Incubation 28 days; fledging 45 days. One brood.
Read: *Ducks of Britain and Europe*, M. A. Ogilvie, Poyser, 1975.

Mandarin *Aix galericulata*

An exotic dabbling duck which has escaped from waterfowl collections to flourish nearby in areas of Surrey, Berkshire and elsewhere.

Surface and up-ending feeders on vegetation, but mainly graze ashore. Will come to corn on lawn. If wood pigeons make their lives impossible, try offering it in the pond.

Nest in tree holes, mostly oak and ash, usually 5 to 24ft (1.5 to 7.2m) above ground.

Nestbox: Upright box, 20in (50cm) high, 8–10in (20–25cm) wide and deep with a 4in (10cm) entrance hole (any shape). Fix at 15ft (4.5m) height, but can be lowered in subsequent seasons if successful.

Eggs: 9–12 eggs in March, hatch in May, one brood.

Gadwall *Anas strepera*

Breeding bird in Britain since mid-nineteenth century, having been introduced to East Anglia. Scattered over British Isles, breeds by shallow, lowland sheets of freshwater, lakes, meres, reservoirs, marshes and slow-flowing streams. Spreading slowly.

Food: mostly vegetable, some animal.

Nest site is concealed in dense vegetation close to water, tussocky grass, sedge, nettles.

Artificial nest site: May nest on rafts, if provided with good growth of vegetation.

Eggs: 8–12 creamy-buff. May or early June. Incubation 27–28 days; fledging 7 weeks. One brood.

Mallard *Anas platyrhynchos*

Generally distributed, near all kinds of freshwater, estuaries and coastal islands.

Food: mainly vegetable. Enjoys soft potatoes.

Nests in thick undergrowth sometimes far from water. Pollard willows, tree holes, second-hand crow nests, etc. Grass, leaves, rushes, feathers, down.

Male Blackbird

Fieldfare

Redwing

Female Blackbird

Song Thrush

Mistle Thrush

These drawings may help to clear up confusion in cases where different species look somewhat similar

Male Greenfinch

Male Siskin

Dunnock
(Hedge Sparrow)

Female
House Sparrow

Adult
Robin

RG

Juvenile
Robin

Nestbox: Try providing an apple-box or large, open cat basket in typical nesting area. Where mallards have become very tame (village ponds and the like), try erecting an open-ended barrel on an island. Otherwise a mere hollow in the ground, bordered by a couple of short logs and sheltering under a wigwam of spruce boughs, may do the trick. Mallard nests are probably best sited on rafts or islands, where they enjoy some protection from foxes and rats.

Alternative nestbox: Using sawmill offcuts, make a box with inside dimensions of 1ft (30cm) square and 9in (23cm) high. Prime with an inch or two (25 to 50mm) of woodshavings. Make a funnel about a foot (30cm) long leading to an entrance hole 6in (15cm) square. This tunnel entrance serves to deter crows. A ramp should lead gently down from the tunnel entrance to the ground. This ease of access is important, not only for the comfort of the duck, but because she might take broods back to the safety of the box at night for the first couple of weeks after leaving the nest, especially in cold weather. The duck likes to be able to see out from the nestbox so provide a horizontal slit in the side.

Eggs: About 12 greyish-green or greenish-buff, occasionally a clear pale blue. February onwards. Incubation 4 weeks; fledging 7½ weeks. One or two broods.

NB: A duck-box may well be taken over by moorhens.

Duck, Tufted *Aythya fuligula*
Local but fairly widely distributed, except in the south-west. Lakes, lochs and reservoirs.
Feeds mostly on insects, molluscs, frogspawn, tadpoles and frogs, and some aquatic vegetation.
Nests close to water in tussocks of sedge or rushes.
Artificial nest-site: May occasionally nest on rafts.
Eggs 6–14 greenish-grey. Second half of May, June. Incubation 23–26 days; fledging 6–7 weeks. One brood.

Eider *Somateria mollissima*
Resident, breeding round Scottish coast, the north-east and north-west (non-breeders further south in summer). Rocky and sandy coasts, sea-lochs and estuaries, hugs coast, seldom inland.
Feed in company, shallow dives for seaweed, crabs, shells.

Like to nest by something, so offer them a stick or a fish-box.
Nest lining of eiderdown.
Eggs: 4–6 large cream eggs. End May, beginning June.
Incubation 4 weeks. Young join crêches and fledge at 2
months.

Goldeneye *Bucephala clangula*
Established in Scotland and increasing with many of those
present using nestboxes.
Food: small invertebrates.
In Scandinavia, goldeneyes nest in tree holes and stumps,
beside lakes and ponds in thickly wooded country. In the late

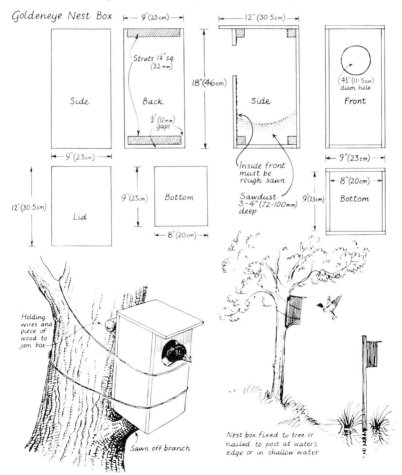

Goldeneye Nest Box

Struts 1¼" sq. (32 mm)

½" (12mm) gaps

18"(46cm)

9"(23cm)

12"(30.5cm)

Side   Back   Side   Front

(4½"(11.5cm) diam hole

Inside front must be rough sawn

Sawdust 3–4"(72–100mm) deep

12"(30.5cm)

9"(23cm)   Bottom   9"(23cm)   Bottom

8"(20cm)   8"(20cm)

Lid

Holding wires and piece of wood to jam box

Sawn off branch

Nest box fixed to tree or nailed to post at water's edge or in shallow water

101

Blackbird sitting tight; please note the implied invitation in the Gas Board's description of the meter (*Brian Hawkes/NHPA*)

Herring gulls have discovered that rooftops make a good substitute
for cliff-slopes (*Tony Soper*)

Middle Ages they were farmed for eggs by Lapps who
improved natural nesting-sites.

Nestbox: Like most hole-nesters, from blue tits to tawny
owls, goldeneyes take readily to artificial nests. They returned
to breed in Scotland in 1971, using boxes which had been first
erected twenty years before. Scottish highland lochs offer
ideal habitat, but nest sites are scarce in the wild, so the RSPB
has erected about 400 boxes and others have been erected by
birdwatchers and foresters. More boxes will benefit this bird.
Materials are as follows: Rough sawn timber 9in wide and
½in thick (230 × 12mm) cut in 9ft or 6ft (274.5 or 183cm)
lengths. Cut the lengths from the saw mill into three different
sizes – work out the correct ratio for the number of boxes to
be constructed. The lengths are 18in (46cm) for the sides, 8in
(20cm) for the bottoms and 12in (30.5cm) for the lids (see
diagrams). Also required are lengths of 1¼ × 1¼in (32 ×
32mm) rough wood cut into 8in (20cm) lengths for strength-
ening inside the boxes. The box is nailed together. Cut 4½in

(115mm) diameter entrance holes after construction by using an electric drill and an electric fretsaw. Finally, cover the lid with 12in (30.5cm) wide bitumastic flashing (as used for finishing off a tarred roof) which you can buy in rolls from builders' merchants. The flashing is burnt onto the box with a blow-lamp and the sides are folded down to cover all the joints. The boxes can be treated with Cuprinol or creosote (if the latter, they need to be treated well before use). It is important that the inside of the box is rough wood and not smooth or else the ducklings cannot get out easily. There is no need for a landing perch; like tits, the ducks fly straight in.

Initially boxes should be erected on trees facing open water at a height of about 10–20ft (30.5–61m) from the ground although they can be used as low as 3ft (9.2m). The RSPB has tended to use places which are not in direct sunlight in the middle of the day and some of the boxes can be up to 30yd (27.5m) from the edge of the water so long as there is a reasonable view and flight path from the water. Once birds have started to nest, new boxes can in fact be up to ½ mile (75m) from the water as the ducks are very good at finding nesting holes and also at leading their young to the water.

Boxes should be well spaced out and erected in small groups of 3–4 boxes; there should not be too many boxes in one area as this leads to increased competition for nest sites and may result in desertion. Quiet undisturbed bays are best but it is also worth using river banks and islands. Use a ladder to put up boxes in trees which are difficult to climb, to save them being looked into by everyone who passes by. Choose quiet areas. In pine marten localities, it is best to use trees on islands or growing in wet areas.

Attach boxes firmly to the trees. One of the best materials is old telephone cable. Wind it around the top and bottom of the boxes and round the tree and then tension by jamming a piece of branch behind the box. This also allows you to slant the box at an angle so that the rain can run off the lid quickly. It may be useful to cut off a branch about 6in (152mm) from the trunk to rest the box on before tying it to the tree.

Put about 3in–4in (72–100mm) of sawdust into the bottom of the boxes – the birds will not use the boxes without adequate sawdust. Goldeneye ducks usually lay their eggs in April/early May and the first young usually appear on the water in May/early June. The birds should not be disturbed while they are incubating (the species is on Schedule 1 of the Bird Protection Act). A check can be made to see if any of the boxes have been used by goldeneye (there will be down and egg-shells in the nest). All boxes should be checked in late winter so that they can be fastened if they have become loose. Sometimes boxes are used by jackdaws which carry sticks into them and these need to be cleaned out annually. Perseverance is required as goldeneye sometimes take a long time to move to new areas.

NB The goldeneye boxes have been developed by Roy Dennis (Highlands Officer of the RSPB) and he welcomes information on their success (Munlochy, Ross & Cromarty, IV8 8ND).

Eggs: 6–15 bluish-green. Mid April on. Incubation 26–30 days; fledging 57–60 days. One brood.

Sparrowhawk   *Accipiter minus*
May visit bird table to sample small birds. Be philosophical! Sparrowhawks have to make a living!

Merlin   *Falco columbarius*
Partial migrant. Open moorland with some trees, coastal dunes and cliffs.

Feeds on small birds, some insects and small mammals. Might be seen chasing small birds near bird table if you're lucky.

Nests on ground among heather or on sand or in old crows' nests. Will take to introduced 'crow' nests in trees at edge of open heather moorland.

Eggs: 2–3 yellowish-brown, speckled reddish-brown. Late May to late June. Incubation 28 days; fledging 4 weeks.

Osprey   *Pandion haliaetus*
Takes freely to cartwheels or ledges on top of tall poles in USA. Roy Dennis, RSPB's Highlands Officer, has had some success in 'gardening' conifers to provide an open platform some 6ft (2m) in diameter. Main problem is vandalism and egg-thieves, so try it only in well-protected areas.

Kestrel   *Falco tinnunculus*
Resident, generally distributed, except in winter in far north.

Moors, coast, farmland and open woodland, suburbs and cities.

Perches on trees, posts, wires or buildings, watching out for its prey. Hunts in the open, checking frequently to hover in characteristic attitude, watching for beetles or small mammals. Untypically, has been known to come to a bird table in hard weather for broken dog-biscuit.

Makes no nest, but uses a scrape on cliff or quarry ledge or uses secondhand crow nest as platform. Sometimes in tree hollow or ledge on building or ruin.

Nestbox: Open-fronted, 25 × 15 × 15in (63.5 × 38 × 38cm) high, with roof overhanging a couple of inches (5cm). One of the long sides is partly open, having only a 5in (12.5cm) board along the bottom part, fitted with a broom pole lip to enable the bird to perch easily before entering. Prime the box with some peat mould or woodshavings. Fix very firmly on 18ft to 30ft (6m to 10m approx) pole, or high on side of house where some shelter is available from midday sun. If fixed to tree, make sure chick thieves cannot climb to it easily, and place it so that wing-exercising juveniles can step out

Finches prefer seeds, and appreciate help towards the end of winter and in early spring when they are hard to find (*John Clements*)

Most birds sip, then raise their heads to swallow, but pigeons (this is
a wood pigeon) keep their heads down and suck up a good draught
(*E. A. Janes/NHPA*)

onto a branch (or extend the broom pole). Swiss-erected boxes were positioned near farm buildings, and in one year no fewer than 26 out of 36 were occupied in an area of about 5,000 acres. With the continuing loss of hedgerow hollow-tree sites it is much to be hoped that these boxes will become more popular with farmers. But it makes a conspicuous nest site, and unfortunately young kestrels have a ready, though illegal, market, so be very careful that they are well

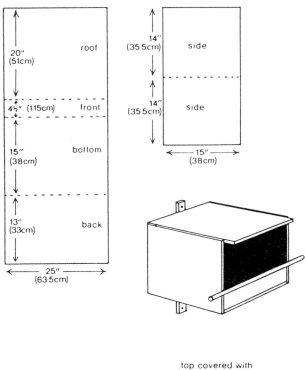

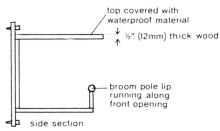

Kestrel boxes have been highly successful

protected. Farm buildings, private parkland, nature reserves and sewage farms are ideal sites. In Holland, where farmers encourage kestrels in controlling voles and shrews, the boxes have been highly successful.

Little owl, jackdaw, collared dove, stock dove or blackbird may also use them.

Eggs: About 5, the white colour often hidden by red-brown splotchings. Mid April onwards. Incubation 28 days; fledging 28 days. One brood.

Pheasant *Phasianus colchicus*
Resident and generally distributed except in Ireland. Much-preserved as a game bird. Woodland edge, cultivated land, parkland, large secluded gardens and shrubberies, damp, rushy and sedgy fields.

Forages on ground for varied selection of animal and vegetable food. Fruit, seeds, grain, insects, worms, slugs. Will come to secluded garden ground station for corn.

Nests under cover of ferns, brambles, etc, in woods, copses, hedgerows and reed-beds, making a hollow in the ground and lining it with a few stems of grass and dead leaves.

Eggs: 8–15 olive-brown eggs. Early April onwards. Incubation 22–27 days; fledging 12–14 days. One brood.

Moorhen *Gallinula chloropus*
Generally distributed, scarcer in northern Scotland. Almost any freshwater from a ditch to a lake; fresh-water ponds, slow streams, marshes and water-meadows.

Forages on grassland and waterside vegetation. Food is mostly vegetable, but includes a fair proportion of animals, such as worms, slugs, and snails. Will soon get used to coming to scraps on the ground; flies less readily up on to the bird table. Watch out for rats.

Nests typically in shallow, still water. Platform of dead plants amongst aquatic vegetation, in trees and bushes.

Nestbox: Will happily take over a duck box, or a mini-island.

Eggs: 5–11 whitish-grey to buff or greenish eggs. April onwards. Incubation 19–22 days; fledging 6–7 weeks. Usually two broods, frequently three.

Read: *A Waterhen's Worlds*, by H. Eliot Howard, Cambridge University Press, 1940.

Young starling and house sparrow. Juvenile plumages can be confusing – young starlings may be mistaken for exotic thrushes; the adult's bill is yellow at courting time (*Mike Read/Swift Picture Library*)

Coot *Fulica atra*
Generally distributed, except in highlands. Lakes, large ponds, slow-flowing rivers and backwaters.
Food: aquatic vegetation, also grazes on land.
Nest is large platform of vegetation built up well above water level, among reeds or in open.
Artificial nest site: Has regularly nested on rafts.
Eggs: 6–9 stone-coloured, spotted dark brown. Second week March onwards. Incubation 21–24 days; fledging about 8 weeks. One, sometimes two, occasionally three broods.

Turnstone *Arenaria interpres*
Winter visitor to rocky or pebbly coasts, although many non-breeders stay for the summer.
Roots about in small parties over rocks or shore, searching for

Birds need water for bathing as well as drinking: (*above*) song thrush; (*below*) young blue tits (*Walter Murray/NHPA*)

small seashore animals in weed and tide-line debris. Comes eagerly to regular beach feeding station for bread, cake, peanuts and scraps in South Devon, and I suggest others should try the experiment. (Winwood Reade tells me that turnstones also come to feed outside the army camp kitchen on the remote island of St Kilda.)
Breeds from Arctic Circle to points north.

Herring Gull *Larus argentatus*
Resident, generally distributed along coasts, estuaries, waters and fields often far inland.
Opportunist feeder, eating almost anything, but mostly animal food. Will come to bird table or ground station for almost anything, but is shy and not particularly welcomed by other birds.
Nests in colonies on cliff ledges, grassy coastal slopes, sand dunes and shingle. Large nest of grass or sea-weed. Of recent years it has taken to nesting on roofs and chimney pot areas where scraps are freely available. Not to be encouraged, though, as it can be aggressive in defence of its young.
Eggs: About 3 eggs, olive to umber, sometimes pale blue or green, splotched with deep blackish-brown. End April to early June. Incubation 26 days; fledging 6 weeks. One brood.
Read: *The Herring Gull's World*, Niko Tinbergen, Collins, 1953.

Black-headed Gull *Larus ridibundus*
Resident and widely distributed. Coastal and inland species frequenting lakes, sewage-farms, harbours and farmland.
Feeds around low-lying shores and estuaries, freely inland to farms, lakes and rivers. Food very varied, animal and vegetable. Will come fairly freely to bird feeding stations in open situations.
Nests in colonies among sandhills, sandbanks, lake islands and shingle. Rough nest of vegetable matter.
Eggs: About 3 eggs, light buffish-stone to deep umber brown, splotched dark blackish-brown. Mid-April onwards. Incubation 22–24 days; fledging 6 weeks. One brood.

Kittiwake *Rissa tridactyla*
Nests in colonies on precipitous sea-cliff ledges. Has enjoyed

man's hospitality by colonising cliff-ledge-like warehouse window-ledges (from 4 pairs in 1949 to 72 pairs in 1978 in North Shields docks).

Tern, Common *Sterna hirundo*
Breeds colonially round most of British coast and inland in Scotland and Western Ireland.
Food: mainly sand eels. Has been known to take bread in company with gulls feeding in the wake of a ferry (Torpoint, Devonport).
Nests in low-lying sandbanks or shingle beaches, low rocky islets and skerries. Inland on islets in lochs and low moorland, river shingle banks.
Artificial nest site: Has nested on rafts. The Merseyside Ringing Group moored a raft on a reservoir belonging to the British Steel Corporation (details on page 39). While the surroundings might have been incongruous, the raft was effective in providing a nesting place and an old-established ternery was able to maintain its presence, thus reversing a trend towards decline. To be worth all this effort, though, the raft must be close to a food source for the terns.
Eggs: Usually 3 stone-coloured. Late May or early June, in a hollow. Incubation 21–28 days; fledging 4 weeks. One brood.

Dove, Rock *Columba livia* (Feral pigeon)
Resident, but decreasing in numbers and hopelessly interbred with its own descendants, the domestic pigeons. The only pure rock doves that remain are probably to be found on the north and west coasts of Scotland and Ireland. Found by rocky sea cliffs and coastal fields, foraging on coastal pastureland for grain, peas, beans, potatoes, seeds, etc. The feral pigeon breeds freely in cities and places where it can take advantage of man's soft heart and kitchen scraps.
Nests in sea-caves or among rocks at wilder parts of coast. Few bits of heather or roots in a hole or cave ledge or crevice.
Nestbox: This species was domesticated hundreds of years ago in Scotland. Artificial nesting ledges were provided for them in convenient sea-caves, and the resulting squabs farmed for food. The flourishing domestic form (feral pigeons) has confused the wild status of the bird in no

uncertain terms. But whether you are dealing with street pigeons or fantails the principles of nestboxing are the same. Pigeons are happiest in a dark chamber which recalls the cave crevices of their ancestors. A garden dovecot, round or octagonal, should be mounted on a stout pole to discourage cats and rats. A two-storey structure makes sense, allowing a number of pairs to breed in companionable proximity. The 'pigeon holes' should provide chambers roughly 24 × 18 × 18in (60 × 45 × 45cm) high, with an entrance hole 6 × 6in (15 × 15cm). The house should be draught-free, but well ventilated, and there should be a generous landing shelf outside the entrance holes (unlike blue tits, pigeons *do* like to land outside the entrance). A roof should keep rain off and also slope south, providing a warm place for the birds to sunbathe and posture.

Eggs: 2 white. April onwards. Incubation 17–19 days: fledging 4–5 weeks. Two or three broods, maybe more.

Dove, Stock   *Columba oenas*
Resident and well distributed, except in northern Scotland. Open parkland, wooded country, cliffs and sand dunes.
Feeds over fields and open ground, taking vegetable leaves, beans, peas and grain.
Nests in holes in old trees, rocks, rabbit burrows, buildings. Insubstantial structure of few twigs, bits of grass, or nothing at all.
Nestbox: Enclosed, with 8in (20cm) diameter entrance hole. 15in (38cm) interior depth, 15 × 25in (38 × 63.5cm) floor. Provide a landing platform. May take to a tree-mounted kestrel box.
Eggs: 2 creamy-white. Incubation 16–18 days; fledging 28 days. Three, four or even five broods.

Wood Pigeon (Ring dove)   *Columba palumbus*
Resident and generally distributed except in extreme north of Scotland. Open country of all kinds, provided there are some trees.
Feeds mainly on ground, but in spring will graze over foliage, buds and flowers in trees. Main food vegetable, cereals, roots, beans, peas and seeds. Will come to garden feeding station for ground food, bread, vegetable scraps, seeds, and may even

visit the bird table. Partial to beans and peas.

Nests in tall hedgerows, almost any kind of tree, second-hand crow nests and squirrel dreys. Sometimes on ground or on building ledges in towns, where it has overcome shyness. Few twigs (you can often see the outline of the eggs if you stand under the flimsy nest).

Eggs: Normally 2 white eggs. April to September. Incubation 17 days; fledging about 3 weeks. Three broods usually.

Read: *The Wood Pigeon*, R. K. Murton, Collins, 1965.

Collared Dove   *Streptopelia decaocto*

Resident and widely distributed. Vicinity of farm-buildings, park-like places and gardens in towns and villages. As recently as 1954 this species did not figure on the British List, yet it is now found throughout the country, the result of a remarkable cross-Europe invasion originating from India.

Finds its food in close relationship with man, sharing grain with chickens, raiding corn and stackyards. In parks and gardens will also take berries and young foliage. Comes freely to bird table and ground feeding station for seeds, peas, grain and scraps,, which may be vital for its survival.

Nests in trees, preferably conifers, on a flimsy platform of sticks, grasses and roots.

Eggs: 2 white eggs. March–October. Several broods.

Owl, Barn   *Tyto alba*

Resident, generally distributed but not abundant and decreasing. Vicinity of farms, old buildings, church towers, etc. Parkland with old timber.

Hunts over fields and open country for small rodents and even small birds.

Nests in ruins or unoccupied buildings, hollow trees and cliff crevices. No material used, the eggs are often surrounded by a pile of cast pellets.

Nestbox: Barn owls are a beneficial species from the point of view of farmers, hunting a diet of short-tailed voles, common shrews and wood mice. Formerly much persecuted by the ignorant, they have been further declining in this century because of habitat loss and human disturbance. But there is also a chronic shortage of suitable nest sites such as old trees, derelict buildings and old-style brick and timber barns. The

115

modern steel-framed barns offer no home to nesting barn owls. Fortunately, they take readily to nestboxes, particularly if the box is placed in a building which is not too often disturbed.

There are several designs, and it may be necessary to use a good deal of ingenuity in fitting the box to the site. The RSPB suggests that enclosed storage barns with access from outside are most favoured, but open Dutch barns are also suitable, particularly if the nestbox can be secured to beams or struts

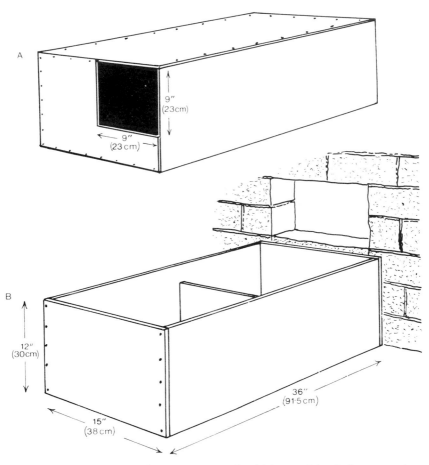

Barn owl nestboxes. Type A should be used in timber-trussed or modern steel-framed barns. Type B is for enclosed storage barns with access from the outside

and used for roosting in winter. This will increase the chance of nesting the following year.

The design of the boxes is quite straightforward, as they can easily be made from a standard tea chest or packing case – both for lightness and ease of conversion they are hard to beat – but the bigger the better. If you can find a source of supply, wooden barrels are also easy to convert. Tea chests and packing cases, however, are not waterproof and should only be sited in dry locations. If the nestboxes are exposed to the elements, more durable and water-resistant material must be used. The lining papers and metal edging around the top of the chest must be removed and any nails knocked flat. You will also need some wooden trays – baker's trays are ideal – which are sawn in half to provide two platforms of about 18in (45cm) in depth. These are important as they provide a safe area in front of the box where the young can come out and stretch their wings.

It is easiest to erect a nestbox in a timber barn – a steel-trussed building may require considerable ingenuity. The most important points to remember are that the boxes must be secure inside the barn, as high above the ground as possible, in the darkest corner out of any draughts and where there is permanent access for the birds. Since height is one of the main criteria, the easiest time for putting up the boxes is when the barn is full of bales. In a timber-trussed barn the box is first nailed, from the inside, front and back to the beam with 3in nails to give a firm fixing. The front which has already had a 9 × 9in (23 × 23cm) opening cut out of the corner, is then fixed to the open end with 1in nails. Finally, the tray is nailed in front of the box. In some cases, it may be necessary to support the platform on timber runners nailed to the underside of the box.

If the barn has steel roof trusses, it is best to nail vertical and horizontal pieces of timber to the box; these can be firmly roped, wired or G-cramped to the steelwork. Every ounce of ingenuity should be used when dealing with these barns, as very often they are the only suitable roosting and nesting-sites for miles around. Boxes can also be placed in corner sites and hung from ridge purlins, but virtually every barn demands its own solution. Barrels can be placed in disused lofts, but here access must be restricted while the birds are nesting.

Whether your boxes are occupied or not, keep the knowledge of their whereabouts restricted to as few as possible. Human predation is, unfortunately, a reality as is disturbance by well-meaning but misguided bird-watchers. Never let any unwanted eyes see you checking a building and only visit occasionally, preferably towards dusk, so that if the adult is inadvertently flushed, it will quickly return. Barn owls are highly sensitive to disturbance. A most important point is that they are included on Schedule 1 of the Bird Protection Act. This means that both the bird and its eggs are specially protected by law, and if you intend to visit your occupied nestboxes you must obtain a special Government Permit. If you see that the box is occupied early in the breeding season, it is probably best to watch from a safe distance, thus avoiding disturbing the birds and the need to become involved in such legalities. The Bird Protection Laws do not hinder the farmer from going about his normal business using the barn! Clear accumulated debris of pellets every year or so.

Eggs; 4–7 white. March–July. Incubation 32–34 days; fledging about 10 weeks. Frequently two broods.

Read: *Owls*, John Sparks and Tony Soper, David & Charles, 1971, 1987.

Owl, Little   *Athene noctua*

Little owls were first introduced to Britain from Italy by Charles Waterton in May 1842, though it was some thirty years later that a similar experiment was successful in the long term. Lack of suitable tree holes may be one of the reasons for their current decline. Resident in southern half of England.

Hunts mainly at dusk and early morning for small mammals, insects and a few birds.

Nests in trees, farm-building holes and rabbit burrows.

Nestbox: Enclosed, at least 4in (10cm) diameter entrance hole, inside depth 12in (30cm), floor 8 × 8in (20 × 20cm). Also may use kestrel box. One of the most successful designs is the 'hollow branch'. Take two round, equal-sized wooden discs of softwood, approximately 2in (5cm) thick and not less than 6in (15cm) diameter. Bore a 2¾in (70mm) entrance hole in one disc. Form a drum by nailing wooden slats 39in × 1in × ½in (1m × 25mm × 12.5mm) to the discs which should be

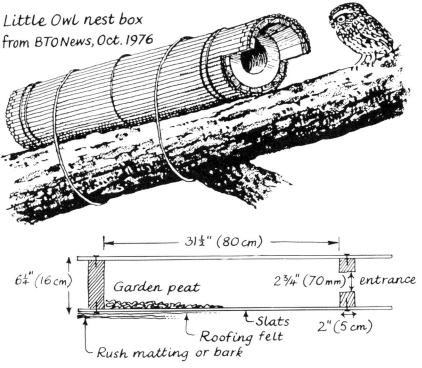

Little Owl nest box
from BTO News, Oct. 1976

31¼" (80 cm)

6¼" (16 cm)　　Garden peat　　2¾" (70 mm) ↑ entrance

Slats

Roofing felt　　2" (5 cm)

Rush matting or bark

31½in (80cm) apart. Secure the drum with wire and wrap it with a layer of roofing felt. Camouflage with a layer of rush mat or loose bark and fasten with wire. Mount on a thick horizontal branch some 10ft to 16ft (3m to 5m) high, the drum sloping slightly to the rear. Don't expose the entrance to the prevailing wind. Prime with garden peat. It is important that the interior is not less than 31½in (80cm) long and the closed end must be light-proof.

Eggs: 3–5 white. April and May. Incubation 28–29 days; fledging about 26 days. Usually one brood.

Owl, Tawny *Strix aluco*
Resident and generally distributed in Britain, but never recorded wild in Ireland. Woodland, farmland, parks and well timbered gardens.

Hunts at dusk for small mammals, birds and insects, even frogs and newts. May take scraps – and small birds – from bird table. May take noctules or pipistrelles in city centre.

Nests in tree holes, second-hand crow, hawk and heron nests, squirrel dreys. Sometimes in barns and on rocky ledges. Branch may need sawing above hole to prevent loss of nest site due to gales.

Nestbox: Enclosed with 8in (20cm) diameter hole at top (see drawing), inside depth 30in (76cm), floor 8in × 8in (20cm × 20cm). Will use a barrel (40gal best, 6gal has been used successfully), if a hole is opened in it and the barrel fixed to a tree crutch about 12ft to 30ft (3.6m to 9m) high, although the height is probably not critical.

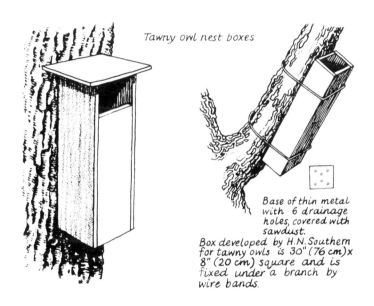

Tawny owl nest boxes

Base of thin metal with 6 drainage holes, covered with sawdust.
Box developed by H.N. Southern for tawny owls is 30" (76 cm) x 8" (20 cm) square and is fixed under a branch by wire bands.

The chimney type nestbox (see drawing) has four wooden planks at least 30in (76cm) long and 8in (20cm) wide butted onto each other, using 2in or 2½in oval nails, to make a square-sectioned chimney. A 9in × 9in (23cm × 23cm) base, which must be perforated by at least half-a-dozen drainage holes, is nailed to one end to form the floor. A thin sheet of ferrous metal is to be preferred to either perforated zinc or a wooden floor. A layer of dry peat or sawdust should be added to the completed base to counteract the fouling that will occur in the fledging period. Chimney boxes of this size are too deep for a hand to reach to the bottom, either for examining, or ringing the nestlings, or for cleaning out. It is practical to make an observation door on one side of the box 8in × 6in (20cm × 15cm), which is hinged to the back of the box and fastened at the front by a hook-and-eye catch. Fit the box under a lateral tree bough at an angle of about 30° from the vertical. If attaching to main trunk, contrive an angle of about 45° to simulate a broken branch. Secure to the tree by wire bands at both top and bottom, but remember these will rust through, or become embedded in bark, so watch your maintenance. In Scotland, box might attract a pine marten.

Eggs: 2–4 white. February to early April. Incubation 28–30 days; fledging about 4 weeks. One brood.

Owl, Long-eared *Asio otus*

Locally distributed over most of British Isles, least common in south-west. Mainly in coniferous woods, plantations, shelter belts; also in well-ivied deciduous woods and marshes, dunes, moorland with low bushes.

Nests in second-hand crow, sparrowhawk, pigeon or heron nests.

Nestbox: Has been known to use duck-type nest baskets in Holland.

Eggs: 4–5 white. March, early April. Incubation 27–28 days; fledging about 23 days. One brood.

Swift *Apus apus*

Summer resident, generally distributed except in north-west Scotland, arriving late April, early May, leaving early August. Habitat exclusively aerial. Rarely on ground except at nest.

Feeds on the wing, taking only insects, anywhere from ground level to 1,000ft.

Nests in colonies, under eaves, in crevices and in holes. Bits of straw, grass, feathers, seed fluff, collected on the wing and stuck together with saliva to form a cup.

Nestbox: Using a plank 65in × 8in × ¾in (165cm × 20cm × 10mm), make a box 19½in × 8in × 5½in (49.5cm × 20cm × 14cm) with an entrance hole cut in the *floor* of the box (not the end, as swifts prefer to enter vertically from below). Make box longer than 19½in (49.5cm) if convenient, but not shorter, as they like to nest at least 1ft (30cm) from the

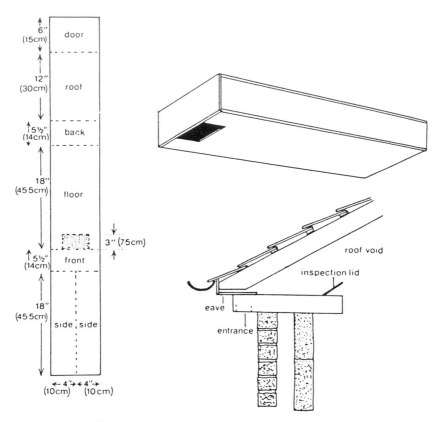

Swift nestbox in place on side of house. By removing a brick or section of wood from the eaves the box may be positioned within the loft with only the entrance hole visible from outside

entrance hole. Prime nest area with a ring of twisted straw. Cut an inspection door 6in × 8in (15cm × 20cm) at rear roof to aid cleaning. Site it under the eaves at least 12ft (3.6m) above ground, up to 100ft (30m) if necessary. Block entrance hole till swifts first arrive, at the end of April or the beginning of May, in order to discourage earlier nesting sparrows and starlings.

Alternative plan: Open out a narrow slit in eaves to allow entrance to roof of your house.

Eggs: 2 or 3 white. Late May, early June. Incubation 18–19

days; fledging about 6 weeks. One brood.
Read: *Swifts in a Tower*, David Lack, Methuen, 1956.

Kingfisher   *Alcedo atthis*
Resident and generally distributed, except in Scotland. Streams, rivers, canals, lakes, estuaries (especially in winter). Perches or hovers above water, fish-watching. Plunges to capture small fish, insects, larvae and amphibians. In winter, visits coast for shrimps, prawns, small rock-pool fish, etc. May come to garden ponds for minnows or sticklebacks.
Nests in tunnels in banks of streams or sand pits, boring 2in (5cm) tunnels as far as 4ft (1.2m) to a nest chamber, preferably in sandy soil.
Artificial nest-site: Will excavate tunnel in artificial bank by suitable stream, a procedure developed by Ron and Rose Eastman. Fix fencing posts eg willow, which will sprout even if embedded in concrete. Stretch 2½in (63mm) mesh chicken wire or square mesh pig wire, to a height of 4ft (1.2m) or more to make a vertical face, facing north if possible, with a degree of privacy and foliage. Fill in behind wire wall with sand or sandy soil. Provide perches and posts nearby. There is no need to cut entrance hole in the netting. The Wildfowl Trust at Arundel in Sussex have had success with this design. Eggs: 6–7 white. Late April to August. Incubation 19–21 days; fledging 23–27 days. Two, three or even more broods.

Hoopoe   *Upupa epops*
Passage migrant, regular in small numbers in spring, less frequent in autumn, on south, south-east and south-west coasts and in east coast as far north as Norfolk. Rare elsewhere in Great Britain. Open woodland, orchards, parkland.
Feeds mainly on ground, often close to human habitation, probing on lawns for insect larvae, etc. Does not often come to bird station, but might do so if mealworms/caterpillars/ant pupae were made available in dish. Not shy.
Normally breeds in Eurasia, but occasionally a hoopoe will nest in one of the southern coastal counties, choosing tree holes, crevices and holes in rough stone walls and ruins.
Nestbox: Uses them on the continent, presumably may do so here.

Eggs: 5–8 whitish-grey or yellowish-olive. May and June. Incubation 18 days; fledging 20–27 days. Two broods.

Wryneck *Jynx torquilla*

Summer resident. Decreasing and scarce in south-east England with a very few pairs now left. However, there are signs of influx to Scotland from Scandinavia, with birds breeding in the Spey Valley, for example.

Picks up insects from tree surface, clinging to trunk like woodpecker. Sometimes on ground, picking up ants, insect larvae. Feeds occasionally at bird tables.

Nestbox: Improve a tree hole. Or try an enclosed box, with a ⅜in × 1¾in (10mm × 45mm) diameter entrance, a 6in (15cm) interior depth, and a 5in × 5in (12.7cm × 12.7cm) floor.

Eggs: 7–10 white. End of May till July. Incubation 12 days; fledging 19–21 days. Usually one brood.

Woodpecker, Green *Picus viridis*

Resident but local in England and Wales, rare in Scotland, none in Ireland. Deciduous woods, parks and farmland.

Searches for insect larvae over tree trunks and branches, probing with long mobile tongue; also feeds freely on ground, especially where there are ants' nests. In times of hard frost, when ant hills are frozen solid, it may damage beehives by boring holes to reach the insects within. May also attack nestboxes. Will visit bird table for mealworms, bird pudding, etc.

Nests in tree trunks, choosing soft or rotting timber, boring a hole horizontally 2in to 3in (5.0cm to 7.5cm) then descending to make a nest compartment over 1ft (30cm) deep and about 6in (15cm) wide at its broadest. Put a few chips at the bottom to form the nest. Sometimes, old holes are used again. Often, starlings take over from them.

Nestbox: Enclosed type with 2½in (63mm) entrance hole, interior depth 15in (38cm), floor 5in × 5in (12.7cm × 12.7cm). Ideal for starlings! Eggs: 5–7 translucent. End of April to May. Incubation 18–19 days; fledging 18–21 days. One brood.

Read: *My Year with the Woodpeckers*, Heinz Sielmann, Barrie & Rockliff, 1959.

124

Great Spotted Woodpecker   *Dendrocopus major*
Resident, widely distributed in England, central and southern
Scotland, none in Ireland. Wooded country – coniferous in
north, deciduous in south – hedgerows, orchards and large
gardens.
Hunts over trees for insect larvae, spiders, seeds and nuts,
even wedging a nut into a tree crack to deal with it. Will come
to bird table for suet especially; also oats, nuts, boiled fat
bacon, hanging fat, or nuts. As adept as tits at feeding upside
down.
Nests in tree holes 10ft (3m) and higher from ground. Few
wood chips form nest.
Nestbox: Enclosed type, entrance hole 2in (5cm), interior
depth 12in, floor 5in × 5in (12.7cm × 12.7cm). Also ideal for
starlings.
Eggs: 4–7 white eggs. May to June. Incubation 16 days;
fledging 18–21 days. One brood.

Lesser Spotted Woodpecker   *Dendrocopus minor*
Resident in southern England and Midlands, becoming local
and rarer further north. Widely distributed but scattered in
Wales. Not in Scotland or Ireland. Same type of country as
greater spotted.
Elusive bird, searching upper parts of trees for insect larvae.
Will come somewhat nervously and rarely to bird table for
fats, nuts and fruit.
Bores nest-hole in decayed soft wood of branch or tree trunk.
A few chips make nest.
Eggs: 4–6 translucent eggs, early May to mid-June. Incu-
bation 14 days; fledging 21 days. One brood.

Skylark   *Alauda arvensis*
Has been known to feed regularly on bread-and-cheese scraps
from a garden of waste ground at the edge of Liverpool. In
hard weather may come to seeds at a ground feeding-station.
In 1977 a pair of skylarks bred on the grassy turf roof of the
visitor centre at the Wildfowl Trust reserve, Martin Mere, in
Lancashire. By 1985 seven pairs had taken up residence on
this high-level and fox-free site.

Martin, Sand *Riparia riparia*

Summer resident, widely distributed. Open country with water.

Feeds mainly over water, taking insects on the wing. Perches on wires and low branches, and will occasionally pick insects from the ground while on the wing.

Nests colonially, digging a long tunnel to a nest chamber, in sand and gravel pits, railway cuttings, river banks and sea cliffs. Few grasses and feathers. Try boring a few enticing 2in (5cm) diameter holes in likely sandbanks, steep road cuttings and banks, especially over water – they may use drainage pipes in a wall which can be deliberately placed for them. A few score breed in this sort of location at the RSPB's Minsmere Reserve in Suffolk, at the car park.

Nestboxes: Near an existing colony, it is worth preparing some underground chambers. Dig a vertical shaft 1ft (30cm) deep, line it with boxing, arrange an access tunnel 2in (5cm) square, from the vertical cliff entrance. The length of the horizontal passage is not critical. Close the nest chamber with a removable lid 6in (15cm) from the floor. Close roof of the shaft with another lid which is concealed by a turf.

Eggs: 4–5 white. Mid May onwards. Incubation 14 days; fledging 19 days. Two broods.

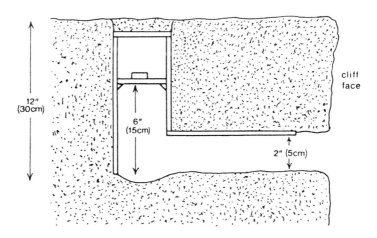

Sand martin nestbox

126

Swallow *Hirundo rustica*

Summer resident, generally distributed. Open farmland, meadows, ponds. Spends much time in flight, especially over water, hunting insects from ground level to 500ft. Unlike swift, settles freely on buildings and wires. Seldom on ground, except when collecting mud for nest.

Nests on rafts and joists, building open mud-and-straw cup, lined with grasses and feathers.

Nestbox: Improvise a simple saucer shape, or fix half a coconut or a 4in × 4in (10cm × 10cm) shallow tray to joist or rafter, even as low as 6ft (1.8m). Will also use specially adapted house martin nestbox placed singly *inside* building. Or, using an old nest, make a plaster of paris mould of the interior. Then take potting clay to make a thick replica, complete with fixing flanges or saddles to fit over a joist, remembering that swallows like to nest against something. Remember to allow continuous access to the nest-site.

Eggs: 4–5 white, spotted with red-brown. Mid May till October. Incubation 15 days; fledging 3 weeks. Usually two broods.

Martin, House *Delichon urbica*

Summer resident, generally distributed.

Habitat as swallow, but more often near human habitation. Hunts insects on the wing, especially over water. Also on the ground.

Originally a cliff nester, has now adopted buildings. Nests colonially on outside walls, under eaves. Cup shape made of mud gobbets with feathers. In dry summer, provide a mud puddle for building material.

Nestbox: Artificial nest from Nerine Nurseries (for address see page 80). Fix under eaves or high window sill. For best results an existing house martin colony should be close at hand. There is some evidence that martins prefer to nest on north and east facing walls. One nest may work, but the more the merrier. Put them in groups outside, under the horizontal or sloping eaves of houses, barns, etc. The artificial cups are held in position by cup-hooks so that it is possible to slide the nest freely in and out to inspect the contents. The entrance hole for house martin nest cups should be no more than 1in (25mm) deep, in order to exclude sparrows. Nevertheless, there have been cases where the hole has been enlarged and sparrows have gained access. There is a method which has been successful in stopping this, based on the fact that martins are able to approach a nest at a much steeper angle than sparrows (see drawing opposite). The hanging cords of the curtain should be no more than 12in (30cm) long and should be fixed to hang 6in (15cm) away from the entrance hole. A spacing of 2½in (63mm) between the cords is effective. Use ⅞in steel nuts as weights on the cord ends. Have all the cords the same length so that they are less likely to tangle in a wind.

One of the objects of using artificial nests is that they frequently encourage house martins to adopt a house not previously 'tenanted' and make their own nests. So, even if the boxes are not used, they may be successful in their purpose. But single nests away from an existing colony are susceptible to attack from sparrows. If the birds try to build and the nests fall off the eaves, a series of nails in the facia board may help with their adhesion.

It is possible to construct your own artificial nest using Polyfilla or a mixture of cement and sawdust. As a model you can use either a plaster of Paris mould of an old nest or a quarter segment of a plastic ball about 7in (17.5cm) in diameter. The Polyfilla or cement mixture should be smoothed over the model to a thickness of about ⅓in (10mm), leaving a flange around the edge to facilitate fixing. The hole should be cut no deeper than 1in (25mm) and no more than 3 to 4in (75 to 100mm) wide. The nest can either be mounted on a board and then fixed up with cup hooks, which allows for easy removal, or it can be fixed directly to the house using Polyfilla. It is often a good idea to smear the outside of the nests with mud, especially around the hole.

Rearing young martins: Occasionally a house martin's nest may fall with the young still inside it. The use of a substitute nest may encourage the parents to continue feeding them. A strong box, deep enough so that they cannot fall out and replaced near the original nest site is usually successful. In one case an old blackbird's nest was used and the parents rebuilt around it. If the parents have deserted, or it is not possible to use a substitute nest, then the young must be fed

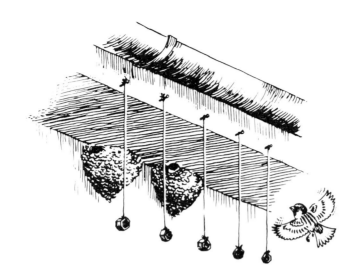

by hand, and if the birds will not feed by themselves they will have to be force-fed using a pair of forceps.

It will be difficult to catch enough insects with which to feed a hungry young martin, but there are a few substitutes. Hard-boiled egg yolk mixed with crushed soaked biscuits provides the necessary nutrients and is similar to the proprietary insectivorous bird food available from pet shops. Cut mealworms and maggots make a good food but a little soaked bread must occasionally be given in order to provide enough calcium. The birds can be fed every two hours, giving them 4–6 maggots or a similar amount of egg mixture.

The birds should be housed in a suitably sized box and kept in a warm place. When ready to fly the best place for them is an aviary where they can practise flying and feeding before release. Fledged birds can be encouraged to feed themselves by threading mealworms or maggots with cotton and suspending them from the ceiling. Care must be taken that the birds do not get tangled in the cotton.

One of the big disadvantages of having house martins nesting on your house (especially over a doorway) is the droppings that will occur beneath the nest. The simplest way to overcome this problem is to fix up a shelf 10in (25cm) wide

about 6ft (1.8m) below the nest, which should catch any droppings. A removable shelf can be made using keyhole brackets. The Wildlife and Countryside Act 1981 now makes it an offence to intentionally take, damage or destroy the nest of a house martin while the nest is in use or being built. Eggs: 4–5 white. Late May to October. Incubation 14–15 days; fledging 19–21 days. Usually two broods, often three.

(*opposite*) Although they commonly patronise continental bird tables, black redstarts are rarities in Britain. This bird, however, took advantage of crumbs put out for it at a dockside canteen in London (*John Flowerday*)
(*below*) The RSPB Gemini feeder offers the bizarre spectacle of a blue tit in a crystal cage (*Martin King/Swift Picture Library*)

Meadow Pipit *Anthus pratensis*
Abundant. Open country, moors, heaths, sand dunes, wintering on lowland pastures, sewage-farms, sea coast.
Feeds mainly on insects, some weeds. Came to ground food-stations of houses estate-built on reclaimed saltmarsh near Bristol, a traditional wintering place. Early winter the most likely time to see it in the garden.

Rock Pipit *Anthus spinoletta*
Resident and generally distributed. Rocky shores in summer; marshes, waterways, estuaries and coasts in winter.
Forages near water for insects, animals and vegetable matter. Will come freely to a ground feeding station near the shore for crumbs, scraps, cheese.
Nests in hole or cliff-crevice close to the shore. Stems and grasses, lined with grass and hair.
Eggs: 4–5 greyish-white eggs spotted olive-brown and ashy-grey. Late April to June. Incubation about 14 days; fledging 16 days. Two broods.

Wagtail, Pied *Motacilla alba*
Resident and generally distributed. Gardens, farms, buildings and cultivated country.
Restless bird, feeds over ground, but often flutters up to take an insect. Mainly insects, fond of shallow pool edges. Will come freely to ground feeding station, scavenging crumbs and scraps where other birds have left unconsidered trifles.
Nests in holes and on ledges of walls, outhouses, creeper, banks and cliffs. Leaves, twigs, stems, lined with hair, wool and feathers.
Nestbox: Ledge or open-fronted box, with a floor area of not less than 4in × 4in (10cm × 10cm). Fix it in a stone wall. Or make a cavity behind a loose stone which can be used as an inspection door.
Eggs: 5–6 greyish- or bluish-white, spotted grey-brown and grey. Late April to June. Incubation 13–14 days; fledging 14–15 days. Two broods. Often host to cuckoo.

Waxwing *Bombycilla garrulus*
Irregular winter visitor, usually to eastern counties.

Food: Hedgerow berries. May come to bird table for fruit in hard weather.

Dipper *Cinclus cinclus*
Resident, generally distributed in suitable localities. Fast-flowing streams and rivers of hills and mountainous regions. Food: aquatic insects.
Nests in wall and bridge holes, rock faces, tree roots and under waterfalls, always close to fast-moving water. Construction of mosses, grasses under an overhang.
Nestbox: May occasionally occupy an open-fronted robin-type box. A German design has been developed to provide nest recesses in the supports of concrete bridges at the time of construction. The essence of the operation is that a recess (see drawing) is left in the concrete by making a mould which is filled with expanded polystyrene and then inserted into the mould for the concrete bridge section. Once the concrete has set, the entrance hole is chipped out and the polystyrene removed. The only remaining task is to fit a front section over the opening. Arrange a suitable perch or dipping stone just above water level if there isn't one already.
Eggs: About 5 white. End of March. Incubation about 16 days; fledging 19–25 days. Usually two broods.

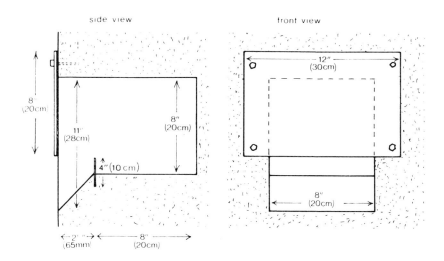

Nest recess for dippers

This RSPB double window feeder offers a choice of seeds or peanuts, but siskins prefer peanuts and fight for them (*Mike Read/Swift Picture Library*)

Nuthatches prefer nuts, the bigger the better – here dispensed by the RSPB's Winter Warmer feeder (*Mike Read/Swift Picture Library*)

The RSPB's dual-purpose nestbox can be changed from enclosed to open-plan by removing the entrance-hole panel, but enclosed nestboxes are by far the most popular; this one is fitted with a metal plate which discourages hole enlargement, a useful anti-woodpecker device (*Mike Read/Swift Picture Library*)

Wren *Troglodytes troglodytes*
Resident and generally distributed. Gardens, thickets, woods, rock banks. Avoids the centres of large towns.
Lives in a world of cracks and crevices, twigs and woodpiles, hedgebottoms, and the mysterious undergrowth round fallen trees. Active and diligent hunter for insects and spiders. Will take crumbs, but is not a common bird table visitor.
Nests in hedges, holes in trees, banks or buildings. Cock bird makes several nests of moss, grass, leaves, etc, and the hen lines her choice with feathers sometimes weeks after the male built it.
Nestbox: May take to a tit box, but is much more likely to find a natural or semi-natural place such as a faggot pile or creeper-clad wall. Excavate a cavity in a bundle of pea sticks or brushwood and lean it against a wall. Provide a coil of rope in the corner of a shed, or hang up an old coat with capacious pocket.
Eggs: 5–6 white, spotted with brownish red. Incubation 14–15 days; fledging 16–17 days. Usually two broods.
Read: *The Wren*, Edward A. Armstrong, Collins, 1955.

Dunnock (Hedge Sparrow) *Prunella modularis*
Resident and generally distributed. Gardens, shrubberies, hedgerows.
Forages unobtrusively on ground among dead leaves, hedgerow bottoms, etc. Weed seeds in winter, insects in summer. Will come freely to ground station, less readily to bird table for crumbs of cornflakes, cake, biscuit, seeds. Unlike most other birds will eat lentils.
Nests in hedges and evergreens, faggot heaps. Twigs, moss, leaves, etc, lined with moss, hair and feathers.
Eggs: 4–5 deep blue eggs. April onward. Incubation 12 days; fledging 12 days. Two broods. Often serves as host to cuckoo.

Robin *Erithacus rubecula*
Resident and generally distributed, except in extreme north of Scotland. Gardens, hedgerows, woods with undergrowth.
Feeds freely in open and in undergrowth. Insects, spiders, worms, weed seeds, fruit, berries. Has a flattering relationship with man and will follow the digging spade hopefully.

Enthusiastic bird-tabler, very fond of mealworms, will also take seeds, nuts, oats, pudding, etc. Fond of butter and margarine, and is alleged to be able to tell the difference! Unsociable bird, it will endure the close company of its relations at the bird table only in hungry times.

Nests in gardens and hedgerows in bankside hollows, tree holes, walls, amongst creeper, on shelves in outbuildings, often at foot of bush or grassy tuft. Foundation of dried leaves and moss, neatly lined with hair and perhaps a feather or two. Nestbox: Ledge or tray, open-fronted box. Interior floor at least 4in × 4in (10cm × 10cm). Old tin, watering can, or kettle, at least quart-size, well shaded from sun, spout down for drainage. Fix it about 5ft (1.5m) up in a strong fork site. Prime with a plaited circle of straw.

Eggs: Usually 5–6 white, with sandy or reddish freckles. Late March to July. Incubation 13–14 days; fledging 12–14 days. Two or more broods.

Read: *The Life of the Robin*, David Lack, Witherby, 1965. *Robins*, Chris Mead, Whittet, 1984.

Black Redstart *Phoenicurus ochruros*
Passage-migrant and winter visitor, some staying to breed in southern England. Cliffs, large old buildings, industrial premises, rocky and 'waste' ground such as building-sites, dumps or ruins.

Restless bird, in trees, over buildings, and on ground. Hawks for insects. Also takes berries. Although it lives amongst us, it is independent of our food, yet surely it might come to a feeding station for minced meat or berries, especially in hard weather.

Nests in crevices and holes of rocks or buildings, or on rafters, under eaves in outbuildings. Loosely-made of grass, moss, fibre, etc, lined with hair and feathers.

Eggs: 4–6 white eggs. Early April onward. Incubation 12–13 days; fledging 16–18 days. Two broods.

Redstart *Phoenicurus phoenicurus*
Summer resident, widely distributed but local. Woodlands, parks, bushy commons with old trees, ruins, orchards, well-timbered gardens.

Restless bird, flitting amongst branches or hawking for

Great spotted woodpecker

Lesser spotted woodpecker

Great spotted woodpeckers can become enthusiastic bird table customers; lesser spotted woodpeckers are more elusive

Bird bells offer a useful method of providing fat-rich pickings for acrobats

The tit family; colour variations in the plumage of closely-related species

Great Tit

Blue Tit

Coal Tit

Long-tailed Ti

Marsh Tit

Willow Tit

RG

insects. Might come to bird table for berries, fruit and mincemeat. Regular visitor to canteen door at Millwall Dock in East London in severe weather for grated cheese, mashed potato and cat food (after the cat had finished).

Nests in holes such as tree or stump, buildings, walls, outhouses, rocks, quarries. Nest made of grass, strips of bark, mosses, roots, and lined with hair and feathers.

Nestbox: Enclosed with entrance hole 1⅛in to 2in (29mm to 50mm) diameter, inside depth not less than 5in (12.5cm), and floor not less than 4in × 4in (10cm × 10cm). Make sure there is a perch not far away from the box (but not on it).

Eggs: About 6 pale blue. May onwards. Incubation 14 days; fledging 14 days. Sometimes two broods.

Wheatear *Oenanthe oenanthe*
Summer visitor, locally common in open country, loose boulders and scree, rabbit warrens, moorland, highland roads, chalk downs, sandy commons and sand dunes, stony shores, rocky islands.

Food: insects.

Nests under a boulder or stone, in rabbit burrow or stone wall. Grass and moss, linings of rabbit fur, feathers, wool.

Nestbox: Has nested under tin cans and in tunnel-type prefabs made of bricks sunk in the shingle at Dungenness Bird Observatory. Be careful to protect the chamber from excessive sunshine, by piling soil or gravel over any metal parts. Likes a few strategically placed twig perches on the flight path to box.

Eggs: Usually 6 pale blue. Late April or May. Incubation 14 days; fledging about 15 days. One brood.

Blackbird *Turdus merula*
Resident and generally distributed. Woods, hedges, gardens, shrubberies.

Feeds in open and in undergrowth, but never far from cover. Makes surprising amount of noise as it searches among dead leaves for insects, worms (which it often steals from a songthrush), fruit, berries and seeds. Will come freely to ground station and to bird table, for sultanas especially, cheese, fat, apples, cake, 'Rice Krispies', berries, seeds.

Nests in hedges, bushes, evergreens, ivy, sometimes in

outhouses. Sturdily built of grasses, roots, etc. Inner mud cup lined with grasses.

Nestbox: Tray or open-fronted, with a floor area 12in × 12in (30cm × 30cm). Or try an inverted cone made of roofing felt. Cut into circle 9in (23cm) in diameter. Cut out and reject a V-shaped sector from centre to a 2in (5cm) arc at periphery. Cut a 1in (2.5cm) section from centre (to provide drainage). Now overlap open ends 3in (7.5cm) and staple strongly. Resulting cone is approx 7in (17.5cm) in diameter with a depth of 2in (5cm). Or try a bundle of pea sticks arranged with a central cave.

Eggs: 4–5 bluish-green, freckled with red-brown. February (or even earlier) to July. Incubation 13–14 days; fledging 13–14 days. Two or three broods, the first often being vandalised because it is insufficiently concealed by leaves, later broods being more successful. Five broods have been raised in one season.

Read: *A Study of Blackbirds*, D. W. Snow, Allen and Unwin, 1958.

Fieldfare *Turdus pilaris*

Winter visitor, generally distributed. Open country, field and hedges.

Flocks feed in open formation across fields, looking for slugs, spiders, insects. In hedgerows, for berries of hawthorn, holly and rowan, yew, etc. In hard weather will come to ground station or bird table for berries, fruit, seeds, pudding, etc. Breeds in Scandinavia, Central and Eastern Europe and Siberia.

Song Thrush *Turdus ericetorum*

Resident and generally distributed. Parks, woods, hedges, shrubberies and gardens, especially around human habitation.

Forages in open and in undergrowth for worms, slugs and especially snails, which it smashes on 'anvil' stones. Also insects, windfalls, berries and seeds. Will eat soft fruit, but is beneficial on the whole. Somewhat nervous visitor to ground station, not so often on bird table; fond of sultanas, also currants, cheese, fat, apples and scraps.

Nests in hedgerows, bushes, trees, among ivy, occasionally in

Titboxes do not need to be made by a cabinet maker with top-quality timber! Great tits are the most enthusiastic of all nestbox occupants (*E. Breeze-Jones/Bruce Coleman Ltd*)

Not only squirrels but foxes and deer may come to your bird tables; grey squirrels are probably the most persistent offenders (*Jeffrey Taylor*)

buildings. Strongly built of grasses, roots, etc. Stiffened with mud and with a unique lining of rotten wood or dung mixed with saliva and moulded into shape by the hen's breast.
Eggs: 4–5 eggs, blue with greenish tinge, spotted black or red-brown. March to August. Incubation 13–14 days; fledging 13–14 days. Two or three broods.

Redwing *Turdus musicus*
Winter visitor, generally distributed. Open country and open woods.
Feeds in loose flocks in fields or woods. Worms, slugs, snails, insects. Hawthorn, holly, rowan, yew berries. In hard weather will come to ground station or bird table for berries, seeds, scraps, fruit, etc.
Breeds in Scandinavia, Eastern Europe and Siberia.

Mistle Thrush (Stormcock) *Turdus viscivorus*
Resident and generally distributed, except in high mountains and treeless districts. Large gardens, orchards, woods.
Feeds mainly on ground, although it likes to sing from the highest point of a tree. Thrives on berries and fruit without conflicting with gardeners' interests. Yew and rowan especially, but also hawthorn, holly, mistletoe, juniper, rose and ivy. All wild fruits except blackberry. Will come to ground station, less freely to bird table for sultanas, currants, and bird pudding. Partial to bird garden life without being particularly friendly to man.
Nests usually in tree fork or on bough. Grasses, moss, etc. Strengthened with earth and lined with fine grasses, the rim ornamented with lichens, bits of wool, feathers, etc.
Eggs: 4 tawny-cream to greenish-blue eggs, splotched with brown and lilac. February to April. Incubation 13–14 days; fledging 14–16 days. Frequently two broods.
Read: *British Thrushes*, Eric Simms, Collins, 1978.

Blackcap *Sylvia atricapilla*
Summer resident, frequently winters, local but fairly distributed, except in remote north and west. Open woodland, thickly bushy places, gardens with trees.
Active bird, searching in cover for insects, fruit and berries. Not often on ground. Will come to bird table for a wide range

144

of food, including rolled oats, berries, crumbs and scraps, especially in hard weather. Overwintering birds are seen mostly near south coast, south-west peninsula and southern Ireland. Windfall apples are an important food item, but they also take *Cotoneaster*, honeysuckle, and holly berries – ivy berries as a last resort. After a heavy snowfall they may take mistletoe berries, rubbing the berry in order to extract the seed. Apart from thrushes, few birds seem interested in mistletoe berries.

Nests in bushes (especially snowberry), hedgerows, evergreens. Stems, roots and grasses, lined with finer grass and hair.

Eggs: 5 eggs, light buff or stone ground, blotched brown and ashy. Mid-May onward. Incubation 10–11 days; fledging 10–13 days. Often two broods.

Chiffchaff *Phylloscopus collybita*
Summer resident.
Insectivorous bird, may come to bird table for kitchen scraps. Overwintering birds more likely to visit bird table.

Goldcrest *Regulus regulus*
Resident and generally distributed except in remote northwest. Woods, coniferous gardens, hedgerows.
Active and tame bird, which flits from twig to twig searching for spiders and insects. Will come to bird table and to hanging fat.
Nests in thick foliage of conifer. Ball of moss lined with feathers, held together by spiders' webs and suspended from branch.
Eggs: 7–10 white/ochreous eggs, spotted brown. End April to early June. Incubation about 16 days; fledging about 18–20 days. Two broods.

Firecrest *Regulus ignicapillus*
Few resident in New Forest, scarce passage migrant along south coast. Woods, gardens, scrub, bracken.
Habits more or less as goldcrest. Will occasionally take suet or fat from crevices in tree-bark, etc. Has taken bread crumbs from bird table.
Nests in tree- or wall-holes; a loose nest of leaves, bark and

mosses, lined with hair and feathers.
Nestbox: May use tit box.
Eggs: 5–9 eggs, late May. Incubation 12–13 days; fledging about 13 days. Single brood.

Flycatcher, Spotted *Muscicapa striata*

Summer resident, generally distributed. Gardens, parks, woodland edges.

Sits on an exposed perch, flits out frequently to hawk after flying insects.

Nests against wall or on small ledge supported by creeper or fruit trees, etc. Moss and grass, lined with wool, hair or feathers.

Nestbox: Ledge or open-fronted box with at least 3in × 3in (7.5cm × 7.5cm) floor. Likes a clear view from nest, so front wall only 1in (25mm) high, enough to retain nest. Hide one of those bowl-shaped wire flower baskets in dense honeysuckle, primed with some moss. Have a perch not far away.

Eggs: 4–5 greenish-grey, with brown spots. Mid May to June. Incubation 12–13 days; fledging 12–13 days. One brood.

Flycatcher, Pied *Muscicapa hypoleuca*

Summer resident but rather local and absent from south-east England. Particularly in oak woods and alder and birch woods along rivers or streams.

Catches insects in flight by hawking, but also takes them from trees and on the ground. Worms and berries occasionally.

Nests in holes of trees, walls. Bark, leaves, grasses with a lining of fibres and grass.

Nestbox: Enclosed, with entrance hole 1⅛in to 2in (29mm to 50mm) in diameter, inside depth not less than 5in (12.5cm), floor not less than 4in × 4in (10cm × 10cm). Have a convenient perch close to the nestbox, but not on it. Takes readily to boxes, which seem to supply a real need.

Eggs: 4–9 pale blue. Mid May. Incubation 12–13 days; fledging 13 days. One brood.

Long-tailed Tit *Aegithalos caudatus*

Resident and generally distributed except in very barren districts and islands. Thickets, bushy heaths, coppices and hedgerows. Also woods in winter.

Feeds in trees, sometimes on ground, restlessly searching for insects and seeds. Parties visit gardens and bird tables for suet, pudding, bread crumbs, grated cheese etc, especially in hard weather. Has been seen to take peanuts from a hanging feeder.

Nests in bushes, furze or brambles, sometimes in trees. Large egg-shaped nest of moss woven with cobwebs and hair with a lining of many feathers. Entrance hole near top.

Eggs: 8–12 eggs, sometimes unmarked, sometimes a cap of spots or freckles. March/April. Incubation 14–18 days; fledging 15–16 days. Normally one brood.

Read: *Titmice of the British Isles*, J. A. G. Barnes, David & Charles, 1975. *British Tits*, Chris Perrins, Collins, 1979.

Tit, Marsh *Parus palustris*

Resident and widespread in most of England and Wales, but not Scotland or Ireland. Deciduous woods, hedgerows, thickets and sometimes in gardens. Likes to be near woodland and not, as might reasonably be imagined, marshes.

Forages over trees for insects; on ground for weed seeds, beechmast, berries and sunflower seeds. Comes to bird table and hanging devices for food as blue tit.

Nests in holes in willows, alders, sometimes in walls. Moss with lining of hair or down.

Nestbox: As blue tit.

Eggs: 7–8 white, spotted red-brown. End April and May. Incubation 13 days; fledging 16–17 days. Generally one brood.

Tit, Willow *Parus atricapillus*

Resident. Fairly frequent in parts of south-east England, scattered locally elsewhere. Marshy or damp woods, hedges and thickets.

Forages over trees and on ground for insects, spiders and berries. Will come to bird table for seeds, peanuts.

Excavates a nest chamber in soft rotten wood – usually birch, willow, alder or elder. Pad of down mixed with wood-fibre, some feathers.

Nestbox: As for blue tit, but not enthusiastic. Stuff it full of sawdust or polystyrene chips so that the willow tit has to excavate a hole. But a far more successful method is to get a

rotten silver birch or alder trunk about 6ft (1.8m) long and
5in or 6in (12.5cm or 15cm) in diameter, and strap it to a
convenient tree, allowing the bird to finish the job. Cap the
top with polythene so that rain cannot penetrate easily. It
seems that the presence of a suitable rotten tree which they
can excavate is all that is needed to attract them to breed in
an area they visit during winter. Nests are usually between
2ft and 5ft (60cm and 1.5cm) high, averaging 3ft (90cm), so
place the trunk accordingly. Birch is the preferred site, alder
and elder are a poor second.

Eggs: 8 or 9 white, spotted brown-red. Late April and May.
Incubation 13 days; fledging 17–19 days. Probably one
brood.

Tit, Crested *Parus cristatus*

Resident in a few parts of north-east Scotland only. Pine
forests and woods.

Forages mainly on tree trunks for insects, ripe pine cone seeds,
berries. Will come to feed at tit-bell and, sometimes, at bird
table.

Nests in holes or crevices in old and decayed pine stumps, also
in alders and birches and sometimes in fencing posts. Dead
moss lined with hair of deer or hare, sometimes feathers or
wool.

Nestbox: Enclosed, with 1⅛in to 1½in (29mm to 38mm)
entrance hole, interior depth not less than 5in (12.5cm), floor
not less than 4in × 4in (10cm × 10cm).

Eggs: 5–6 white, splotched with chestnut red. End April and
May. Incubation 14–15 days; fledging 17–18 days. One
brood.

Tit, Coal *Parus ater*

Resident and generally distributed. Wooded country and
gardens with a preference for conifers. Not so commonly
found in orchards and hedgerows.

Forages in trees, especially conifers, for insects and spiders.
On ground, for seeds and nuts. Not quite so common at bird
tables as great and blue tits, but will take the same foods.

Nests in tree, wall or bank holes, close to ground. Moss with
thick layer of hair or down and feathers.

Nestbox: As blue tit.

Eggs: 7–11 white, with reddish-brown spots. Late April and May. Incubation 17–18 days; fledging 16 days. Sometimes two broods but usually in different nestboxes.

Tit, Blue *Parus caeruleus*
Resident and generally distributed except in north-west Scotland. Woodland, hedges, gardens.

Forages in trees, hedgerows and around houses. Eats wheat, nuts, seeds and insects. Damage to buds and ripe fruit outweighed by consumption of insects. Pugnacious, will hold insect prey with its feet and dismember with bill almost like a hawk. Confiding species that will come readily to bird feeding stations for almost anything. Hauls peanuts 'beak over claw' in a version of the natural behaviour involved in pulling leafy twigs closer to inspect for caterpillars. Milk-drinker, as great tit.

Nests as great tit. Blue tits may go to a nestbox because the best natural sites have been taken by the dominant great tits. Nestbox: Enclosed, with 1in to 1⅜in (25mm to 30mm) entrance hole, otherwise as great tit.

Eggs: 7–14 (though there is a record of 19!), usually spotted light chestnut. Late April and May. Incubation 13–14 days; fledging 15–21 days. One brood. Blue tits breed most successfully in deciduous woodland, where there is an abundance of caterpillars. Their breeding success is least in built-up areas, even though their clutch sizes are smaller to compensate for the poor food available.

Tit, Great *Parus major*
Resident and generally distributed, scarcer in northern Scotland. Woodland, hedges, gardens.

Forages in trees and hedgerows for insects, spiders, worms. Fruit, peas, nuts and seeds. Does some damage to buds in spring, but it was once estimated that one pair of great tits will destroy 7,000 to 8,000 insects, mainly caterpillars, in about three weeks. Fierce bird that will attack and eat a bee. Comes freely to bird table, to hoppers and scrap baskets, where it will display its acrobatic powers as it takes coconut, peanuts, hemp and other seeds, meat, fat, suet, pudding and cheese. May help itself to cream off the top of your milk bottle if you leave it too long on the doorstep.

Nests in tree or wall holes, or crevices. Also in second-hand nests, or the foundations of larger nests. If no natural sites are available, it may use letterboxes, flower pots, beehives and almost any kind of hole. Nest lined with a thick layer of hair or down.

Nestbox: Enclosed, with 1⅛in (29mm) diameter entrance hole or slightly larger, interior depth at least 5in (12.5cm) from hole to floor, and floor at least 4in × 4in (10cm × 10cm). Great tits are the most enthusiastic customers for boxes, with blue tits coming second. They not uncommonly occupy the same box, the great tits taking over, covering the blue tits' eggs with a fresh lining and hatching only their own eggs (though mixed broods are not unknown). Tit boxes are successful even in woodland, where there is a shortage of old trees because management procedures do not tolerate them. Result is strong competition for sites.

Eggs: 5–11 white, splotched reddish brown. End April to June. Incubation 13–14 days; fledging about 3 weeks. One brood.

Nuthatch *Sitta europae*

Resident and fairly common in Wales and southern England. Old trees in woods, parkland, gardens.

Dodges about on tree trunks. Wedges nuts, acorns, beechmast and seeds in crevices, and hacks them open with bill. Also takes insects. Will come freely to bird table and hanging devices for hemp, seeds, nuts, cake, fat, etc. Try jamming a brazil nut into a crevice.

Nests in tree holes or sometimes in wall hole. Female fills crevice and reduces entrance to desired size with mud. Nest lined with flakes of bark or leaves.

Nestbox: Enclosed, with 1⅛in to 1½in (29mm to 38mm) entrance hole, interior depth not less than 5in (12.5cm), floor not less than 4in × 4in (10cm × 10cm).

Eggs: 5–9 white, spotted with red-brown. End April to June. Incubation 14–15 days; fledging about 24. One brood.

Treecreeper *Certhia familiaris*

Resident and generally distributed. Woodland, parks, gardens with large trees.

Forages unobtrusively for insects over trees. Does not come to bird table, but may indulge in crushed nuts, porridge or suet fat spread in crevices of rough-barked trees, especially Wellingtonia. Has visited peanut feeders. Try uncooked pastry.

Nests behind loose bark or cracks on tree trunks, or behind ivy. Sometimes in wall or building crevices. Twigs, moss, grass, lined with feathers and bits of wool.

Nestbox: May come to conventional enclosed type, but a wedge-shaped box has been specially designed with their needs in mind (see below), though I've had one up for years without success. An alternative design involves a book-shaped box 7¼in (18cm) tall by 4¾in × 1⁹⁄₁₆in (12cm × 4cm), with a 2in × 1in (5cm × 2.5cm) entrance hole at the top of the 'spine'. Clamp it to a tree trunk at around 10ft (3m) high. Or try securing a loose piece of bark to a tree trunk to simulate a natural crevice. Entrance must be alongside tree trunk.

Eggs: Usually white, with red-brown spots at larger end. End April to June. Incubation 14–15 days; fledging 14–15 days. There may be a second brood.

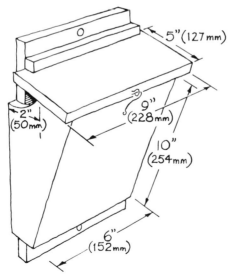

Wedge - shaped box
for Treecreepers

Jay *Garrulus glandarius*

Resident and generally distributed. Woodland, never far from trees.

Hops about branches and on ground. Mostly vegetable food, peas, potatoes, corn, beechmast, nuts, fruit and berries. Animal food includes eggs and small birds, mice, slugs, snails, worms and insects. Eats large numbers of acorns and, like other crows, has the habit of burying acorns and other surplus food in secret places in trees and under ground. Shy bird, except in some well-timbered suburban areas where it becomes very tame and will come to the bird table or ground station for almost any food. Has learnt to shake spiral peanut-holders to dislodge nuts in order to pick them up from the ground.

Nests fairly low in undergrowth or tree-fork. Sticks and twigs and a little earth, lined with roots and perhaps hair.

Eggs: 5 or 6 sage-green or olive-buff eggs, mottled with darker olive spots. Early May. Incubation 16–17 days; fledging 20 days. One brood.

Magpie *Pica pica*

Resident and generally distributed in England and Wales, scarce in parts of Scotland. Farmland and open country with hedges and trees.

Frequently in pairs or small parties foraging on ground and in hedgerows for insects, small mammals and birds. Cereals, fruit, nuts, peas and berries. Will come to bird table or ground station for large scraps, which it takes away. Fond of the milk bottle. Not to be too warmly welcomed because of its predatory habits in the breeding season.

Nests in tall trees, thorny bush or neglected hedgerow. Bulky, domed structure of sticks, with an inner lining of earth and roots.

Eggs: 5–8 eggs, greenish-blue to yellowish and greyish-green, spotted and mottled brown and ash. April onwards. Incubation 17–18 days; fledging about 22–27 days. One brood.

Read: *Crows of the World*, Derek Goodwin, British Museum (Nat Hist), 1976. *Crows*, Franklin Coombs, Batsford, 1978.

Chough *Pyrrhocorax pyrrhocorax*
Resident. Rare, but a stable and healthy population of less than a thousand pairs in the British Isles. Confined to Scotland, Wales and Ireland (the Celtic Crow, sadly none left in Cornwall now).

Nests in crevices or holes in cliffs and sea caves (though often inland in Wales, in disused quarries and in mineshafts). Bulky structure of sticks, heather stalks, etc, lined with wool and hair. Many breed in man-made features such as ruined buildings, castles, bridges, lighthouses etc.

Has been known to use artificial covered nest sites in ruins and such places as Martello towers.

Eggs: 3 or 4 blue with brown spots. Late April onwards. Incubation 17–18 days; fledging about 38 days. One brood.

Read: as magpie.

Jackdaw *Corvus monedula*
Resident and common except in north-west Scotland. Farm and parkland, cliffs, old buildings.

Jaunty bird, feeding in parties or flocks on animal and vegetable matter. Will take young birds and eggs if it gets the chance. Comes freely to bird table or ground station for scraps, cereals, potato, fruit, berries and nuts. Fond of macaroni cheese.

Nests in colonies in trees, buildings, rocks or rabbit burrows, holes, cracks or crevices. Almost any hole will do – often in bottom of rook or heron's nest. Twigs, sometimes very bulky, sometimes not. Lining of grass, wool, hair, etc.

Nestbox: Enclosed type, with not less than 6in (15cm) entrance hole, 17in (43cm) interior depth, and at least a 7½in × 7½in (19cm × 19cm) floor. Or open type as for kestrel.

Eggs: Usually 4–6 pale greenish-blue, spotted brownish black. Mid April. Incubation 17–18 days; fledging 17–18 days. One brood.

Read: as magpie.

Rook *Corvus frugilegus*
Resident and generally distributed. Agricultural areas with trees for nesting.

Feeds openly on ground in small parties or flocks. Cereals, potatoes, roots, fruit, nuts, berries, insects, worms. Will also feed on carrion (dead lambs, etc), and kill small birds in hard weather. Comes freely to ground station for almost anything. Nests in tree-top colonies normally. Mass of sticks solidified with earth, lined with grasses and straw.

Eggs: 3–5 light blue-green to green and grey-green eggs. Late March onwards. Incubation 16–18 days; fledging 29–30 days. One brood.

Read: as magpie.

Starling *Sturnus vulgaris*

Resident and generally distributed. Found almost anywhere, having successfully adapted to man's ways.

Active bird, foraging on ground and in trees and hawking for insects. Animal and vegetable foods of almost any kind. Enthusiastic bird table and ground station visitor. Sometimes defeated by hanging devices, but individuals have even learnt to extract peanuts from mesh bags. Very fond of fresh creamy milk and leg-of-lamb bones, particularly marrow, but will eat anything available.

Nests, often in colonies, in tree or building holes. Untidy structure of straw and grasses lined with feathers.

Nestbox: Enclosed, with entrance hole 2in (5cm) diameter, inside depth 12in (30cm), floor area 9in × 9in (23cm × 23cm).

Starlings will explore many possibilities of piracy, and will sometimes take over an old tit box, when the wood has softened enough to enable them to hack away at the hole and enlarge it. If they annoy you by taking over the nestbox, consider that there may be a great spotted woodpecker nearby who has been spared eviction.

Eggs: 5–7 pale blue. End of March onwards. (They often get taken short and lay one on the lawn.) Incubation 12–13 days; fledging 20–22 days. Usually one brood, two in south-east England.

Read: *The Starling*, Chris Feare, OUP, 1984.

Sparrow, House *Passer domesticus*

Resident and widely distributed. Cultivated land and vicinity of human habitation.

Operates in non-territorial 'gangs', cleaning up wherever there are easy pickings on farms, hedgerows, parks, gardens, docks, railways, and 'waste' land of all kinds. Corn, seeds, insects. Tough customer at the bird table, eating almost anything, especially cereal-based foods. Wastes a great deal. Much too successful; where there are too many sparrows other birds tend to get crowded out. Has learned to extract peanuts from net bags, sometimes even hovering to do so. May hang upside-down tit-style to get at nuts from a 'difficult' feeder.

Nests in holes or niches around occupied houses: eaves, drainpiping, creeper, also in hedges and trees, house martins' nests, or in the foundations of rooks' nests. Untidy structure of straw and grasses lined with feathers and oddments. In cramped locations may consist of lining only.

Nestbox: Enclosed, with entrance hole 1¼in (32mm) diameter, inside depth not less than 5in (12.5cm), floor area 6in × 6in (15cm × 15cm).

May easily become a pest, denying nestboxes to more welcome birds. Drastic solution is to destroy nests as soon as they are built.

Eggs: 3–5 greyish-white, finely spotted grey and brown. May to August. Incubation 12–14 days; fledging 15 days. Two to three broods.

Read: *The House Sparrow*, J. D. Summers-Smith, Collins, 1963.

Sparrow, Tree *Passer montanus*

Resident and widely distributed in England, Wales, eastern side of Scotland and a few parts of Ireland. 'Country cousin' of house sparrow, frequenting same habitat but less attached to human habitations.

Feeds on weed seeds, corn, insects, spiders. Will visit bird table for seeds and scraps but is a shy bird compared with the house sparrow.

Nests in holes of trees, banks, haystacks and thatch, buildings

and in foundations of disused rook or magpie nests. Untidy, similar to that of house sparrow.

Nestbox: Enclosed, with entrance hole 1⅛in (28mm) diameter, inside depth not less than 6in (15.25cm), floor not less than 4in × 4in (10cm × 10cm). Very susceptible to disturbance.

Eggs: 4–6, smaller, browner, darker than those of house sparrow. Late April to August. Incubation 12–14 days; fledging 12–14 days. Two broods usually.

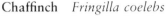

Chaffinch *Fringilla coelebs*
Resident and widely distributed. Gardens, hedgerows, woods, commons, farmland.

Forages on ground and in trees. Insects, spiders, fruit, fruit buds. Tame and enthusiastic bird-tabler, taking seeds of all kinds, bird pudding, scraps and berries.

Nests in hedgerows, orchards, gardens, not choosy. Beautiful structure of moss with interwoven grass and roots, decorated with lichens held together by spiders' webs. Lined with hair and feathers.

Eggs: 4–5 greenish-blue to brownish-stone eggs, spotted/streaked purplish-brown. Mid-April to June. Incubation 11–13 days; fledging 13–14 days.

Brambling *Fringilla montifringilla*
Has been known to take mixed seeds dropped from bird table and peanuts from a mesh bag. Visits bird table in hard weather.

Greenfinch *Chloris chloris*
Resident and common. Gardens, shrubberies, farmland.

Feeds sociably on ground and in trees. Seeds of all kinds, berries, fruit tree buds, occasionally beetles, ants, aphids. Comes to bird table and seed hoppers for sunflower seed especially, but is most enthusiastic about peanuts. Will appear where not previously seen when peanut bag hoisted. Will even eat buckwheat. Berries of yew, ivy, hawthorn, elder, etc. Windfalls.

Nests in hedgerows and evergreen bushes and trees. Moss interwoven with twigs and lined with roots and hair, sometimes feathers.

Eggs: 4–6 eggs, ground colour dirty white to pale greenish-blue, variably spotted red-brown. Late April/May onwards. Incubation 13–14 days; fledging 13–16 days. Two broods.
Read: *Finches*, Ian Newton, Collins, 1972.

Goldfinch *Carduelis carduelis*
Resident and generally distributed. Gardens, orchards and cultivated land.
Small flocks flitter around plant seed-heads, not so much on the ground. Seeds, especially thistle, teazle and other weeds. Also insects. Will come occasionally to the bird table for small seeds of grains and grasses. Crack some hemp for them, as their beaks are not as strong as those of other finches. Have been known to take peanuts from a string.
Nests especially in fruit trees and chestnuts. Also in hedges and thick berberis. Elegant nest of roots, grass, moss and lichens, lined with vegetable down and wool, placed far out at the end of the branch.
Eggs: 5–6 bluish-white eggs, spotted and streaked red-brown. Early May onwards. Incubation 12–13 days; fledging 13–14 days. Two broods.

Siskin *Carduelis spinus*
Resident in parts of Ireland, Scotland and Wales and in Devon, the New Forest and Norfolk. Increasing. Mainly winter visitor, widely distributed. Woods in summer, otherwise copses, streams, gardens.
Seen in mixed parties with redpolls searching spruce, birch and larch for seeds. Since the mid-1960s has become increasingly common in gardens in winter, a habit which spread from Surrey through the south-east. Perhaps first attracted by suitable seed-bearing trees, it has stayed to enjoy the bird table, specialising in meat fat and peanuts. Very tame, seeming almost indifferent to man, though aggressive in behaviour to other birds. Said to be especially attracted to peanuts in *red* mesh bags; one observer found that while red mesh failed, nuts in a *white* RSPB scrap cage did the trick.
Nests in conifers, high up. Moss and wool interwoven with grass and twigs. Lined with rootlets, down and feathers.
Eggs: 3–5 eggs. April to May. Incubation 11–12 days; fledging about 15 days. Two broods.

Linnet *Acanthis cannabina*

Grain-eater, which may come to bird table for kitchen scraps.

Redpoll *Acanthis flammea*

Grain-eater, which may come to bird table for kitchen scraps. Especially in Scotland.

Crossbill *Loxia curvirostra*

Late summer visitor. Varying numbers. Every few years invades and over-winters in great numbers, many individuals remaining to breed. Coniferous woods, gardens and parks.

Clambers about branches parrot-fashion in parties, wrenching off pine and larch cones. Holds cone in foot while it splits the scales and extracts the seed with its tongue. Apart from cone seeds, will eat thistle seeds, berries and insects. Very tame, it will visit bird table for seeds, especially sunflower. Very fond of water and bathing.

Nests on pine branches. Foundation of twigs, cups of moss, grass and wool lined with grass, fur, hair, feathers.

Eggs: 4 greenish-white eggs with few spots/streaks of purple-red. January to July. Incubation 12–13 days; fledging more than 24 days.

Bullfinch *Pyrrhula pyrrhula*

Resident and generally distributed. Shrubberies, copses, gardens, orchards, hedgerows.

In autumn and early winter eats mainly weed seeds, some berries; in a hard winter, if its natural food, ashmast, is short it will ravage fruit tree buds. Remedy is to spread 'Transweb' (Transatlantic Plastics Ltd, Ventnor, IoW) among branches of smaller trees and shrubs. Unsightly but effective. Not keen on bird tables, may occasionally come for seeds and berries, but is especially fond of black and red rape. Will take peanuts from a mesh bag (or from another bird), but cannot extract them from shell.

Nests in hedges, evergreen bushes, creeper, brambles. Foundation of twig and moss, cup lined with interlacing roots and hair.

Eggs: 4–5 green-blue eggs with few purple-brown spots and streaks. Late April onwards. Incubation 12–14 days; fledging 12–17 days. At least two broods.

Hawfinch *Coccothraustes coccothraustes*
Resident, generally distributed, but not much in evidence; local in Great Britain, but very rare in Ireland. Woodland, parks, orchards and wooded gardens.
Feeds in trees, taking kernels and seeds. Fond of green peas. Will come shyly to bird table for fruit, seeds and nuts. Highly-developed bill muscles enable it to crack cherry and plum stones, etc, to extract the kernel.
Nests on fruit tree branches or in bushes and other trees. Foundation of twigs supports shallow cup of lichens, moss, grass lined thinly with roots and hair.
Eggs: 4–6 eggs, ground colour light bluish or greyish-green spotted and streaked blackish-brown. Late April onwards. Incubation 9½ days; fledging 10–11 days. Occasionally two broods.
Read: *The Hawfinch*, Guy Mountfort, Collins, 1957.

Snow Bunting *Plectrophenax nivalis*
Has patronised Scottish bird tables, and vessels of the Royal Navy in northern latitudes.

Yellowhammer (Yellow bunting) *Emberiza citrinella*
Resident and generally distributed. Farmland with hedgerows or bushy cover, bushy commons and heaths. Very common along roadsides.
Feeds mainly on ground, hopping and pecking for corn, weed seeds, wild fruits (including blackberries, which most birds don't like), leaves, grasses. Insects, spiders, worms, etc. Will come to garden seed-hopper once it has discovered it, but not really a garden bird.
Nests in bottom of hedgerow or bush. Straw, grass, stalks, moss-lined with hair and grass.
Eggs: 3–4 eggs, whitish to purplish to brownish-red with dark brown hairlines and spots. Late April to August or later. Incubation 12–14 days; fledging 12 –13 days. Two or three broods.

Reed Bunting *Emberiza schoeniclus*
Resident and generally distributed except in Shetlands. Reed-beds, rushy pastures, marginal land and hedgerows, having expanded recently to add dry country and suburbia to its

ancestral wetland habitat.

In wintertime joins with yellowhammers and finches in open fields and visits gardens, often in early spring, for seeds and crushed oats.

Nests in marshy ground, with thick vegetation, sometimes in bushes. Dried grasses and moss, lined with fine grasses, hair. Nestbox: May take advantage of goose/duck raft and nest on it.

Eggs: 4–5 eggs, bluish. May/April. Incubation about 13–14 days; fledging 10–13 days. Two or three broods.

One or two surprises!
Ring-necked Parakeet (or rose-ringed parakeet) *Psittacula krameri*

This African/Indian species has been colonising the fringes of London since first escaping from captivity (or being deliberately released) around 1969. Now breeding successfully and spreading. Suburban parks, large gardens. Feeds freely at bird tables. Offer it dates, if you can afford them. Nests in tree holes. Presumably it will take to enclosed boxes.

Budgerigar *Melopsittacus undulatus*

Escaped or released cage birds sometimes breed in the wild in the south east. There is an established free-flying colony on the island of Tresco, in the Scillies. These birds, often very tame, will come readily to feeding devices for seeds.

Canary *Serinus canaria*

As budgerigar, will use seed feeders.

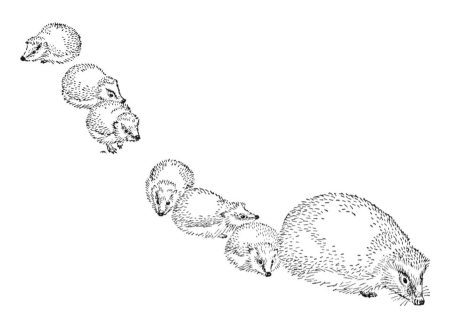

7 Why only birds?

Birds tend to get more than their fair share of attention. Other animals are equally interesting and entertaining, and often equally beneficial to the garden. Take insects, for instance. Most people regard all insects as pests whereas, in fact, only a few hundred out of more than 20,000 British species can reasonably be classified as harmful; by harmful, I mean those that interfere with man's activities, damage crops and so forth. No doubt, the pests themselves would take a different view, and many of the species not only live without encroaching on our lives, but are of great benefit to us. Pollinating bees are an obvious example of how useful insects can be, and a wide variety of flies, beetles, butterflies, moths and wasps also pollinates many flowers. Ladybirds, too, are useful, preying on such harmful insects as aphids and thrips, so if you find a winter colony hibernating in some crevice, leave them in peace. Dragonflies are also useful, eating many other insect species which we regard as harmful. Above all, spiders are useful, eating a great quantity of insects.

Toads are interesting creatures to attract to your garden.

Standard bat box — Construction

Cm	20	9	14	33	20	14	= 111 cm
15cm	Roof	Base	Front	Back plate	Side	Side	6"
in	8	3½	5½	13	5½	7¾	= 43½ in

Plank marking and cutting (note: 1cm allowed
    for saw cuts)

Plank 6" or 15 cm wide × 1" or 2½ cm thick

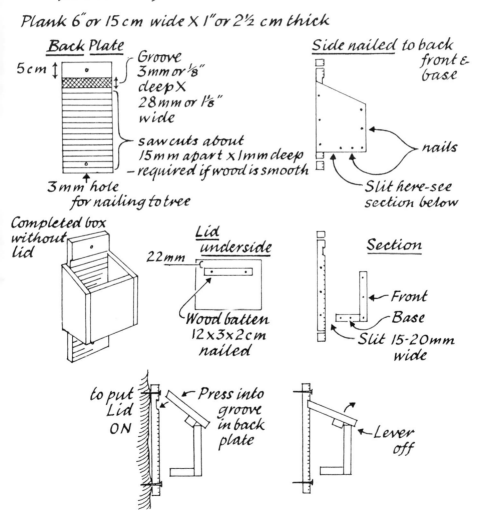

Back Plate

5 cm

Groove
3mm or ⅛"
deep ×
28mm or 1⅛"
wide

saw cuts about
15mm apart × 1mm deep
– required if wood is smooth

3mm hole
for nailing to tree

Side nailed to back
front &
base

nails

Slit here – see
section below

Completed box
without
lid

Lid
underside

22mm

Wood batten
12 × 3 × 2 cm
nailed

Section

Front
Base
Slit 15–20mm
wide

to put
Lid
ON

Press into
groove
in back
plate

Lever
off

Provide a convenient home for one – a hole in a wall, a cavity under a stone or plank – and it may stay with you for years and become a family pet. One naturalist had a toad living under his doorstep for thirty-six years. Toads have a well-developed memory for locality, and though they may forage long distances for food, they will return safely afterwards. They will come out in the daytime in a heavy shower but, normally, they feed in the late evening and early at night. They eat snails, beetles, ants and other insects, caterpillars, woodlice and worms, and will even take snakes and mice.

Bats are much maligned creatures which are much more likely to decimate the flying insects round your house than get tangled in your hair. Their numbers are sadly declining, for various reasons including cave disturbance, rubbish dumping and ill-advised roof fumigation. So you might care to encourage this harmless and useful beast by putting up special nestboxes or by providing a small access-hole to your loft.

Bats use boxes (see drawing opposite) both as roost-sites and as nurseries, so it is important that the internal size is large enough to allow clusters of the animals to develop, since this is their strategy for heat conservation.

Timber should be 1in (25mm) or thicker, and rough-sawn so that the bats may crawl all over the surfaces. If the timber has already been planed then make shallow horizontal saw cuts to offer a grip to the bats' sharp claws. Do not use any paint or preservative.

Fix the box firmly to a tree, high up and with an uncluttered final approach for the bats' flight path. For full details, write to the Fauna and Flora Preservation Society (address page 169) and ask for a copy of 'Bat Boxes'.

Hedgehogs make charming friends and no garden should be without its nightly visit in summer, although I would never suggest keeping one in captivity. Unless your garden is very large, your hedgehog will want to wander a great deal, but if you provide the right facilities it may use your premises as its base. To my mind, this is the most rewarding of all animal relationships. With a captive animal you can never be quite certain that it is content. A free-living, wild creature which chooses to settle with you will give much deeper pleasure, and provide a never-ending source of interest.

Quite apart from their engaging habits, hedgehogs are

*Young Hedgehog
sketched in August*

positively useful. They eat formidable quantities of slugs, millipedes and caterpillars, but not useful insects such as ladybirds, devil's coach-horse and violet ground-beetles. They even eat adders, on occasion, though I would not classify the adder as a pest.

Hedgehogs can be attracted in much the same way as birds. Food must be put out for them and they must be provided with nestboxes. They are nocturnal creatures, coming out to feed at dusk from late March to November (in the winter they hibernate). Put out a saucer of bread and milk for them. They need to have water, too, but your ground-level bird bath will serve very well. Hedgehogs are also fond of tinned salmon, oranges, and tomatoes, as well as the more obvious kitchen scraps.

A most interesting design for a hedgehog nestbox has been developed by the Henry Doubleday Research Association (see *Hedgehogs and the Gardener*, at the end of this chapter) and, with permission, I am reproducing the dimensions and details of their hog-kennels. The box should be about 12in by 15in by about 13in high (30cm × 38cm × 32.5cm), and made of untreated timber. Hedgehogs have a keen sense of smell, objecting to both tobacco smoke and artificial preservatives. To prevent cats getting in, there should be an entrance tunnel a couple of feet long (60cm) and with a 4½in (11.3cm) square section.

It is important that there should be a ventilation shaft, and

164

that air should be able to pass freely through the box; otherwise it will become uncomfortably wet inside. Bear in mind that the hedgehog will probably try to fill the box very full with hay and make sure the ventilation pipe doesn't get blocked. Perhaps the best plan is to make a simple 'baffle' with a fairly tightly rolled piece of chicken wire (see illustration). Fit it firmly so that the hedgehog doesn't dislodge it while he's thrashing about inside. The box needs to be rainproof so cover the roof with a piece of polythene that just overlaps the sides of the box. (Do not seal the box completely with polythene or there will be condensation troubles and the inside of the box will become sodden before its time.)

Cover the whole assembly with at least 1ft (30cm) of earth, so that just the entrance tunnel and feeding hatch are visible. Hedgehogs like to have plenty of dry bedding in their homes, so make some hay or dry leaves available near the box entrance. Put it in a container so that it doesn't get wet and they'll drag it across to the box entrance, leaving some odd bits on the way as evidence.

If there are any hedgehogs in your locality (dead bodies on the road are a certain clue), one may soon discover and adopt your box. Otherwise, you may choose to import one. It is no bad thing to collect hedgehogs found in the road, because they are in danger from passing traffic and you are doing them a

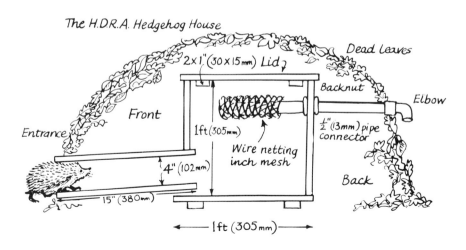

The H.D.R.A. Hedgehog House

165

good turn by rescuing them. However, this should only be done at times when it is unlikely that you are rescuing a female hedgehog which has a nest of babies somewhere. Unfortunately, there is no easy way of sexing hedgehogs. You are safe enough in taking young ones – up to Spanish orange size – at any time, but adults should only be collected in early spring until mid-May, in August, and again from mid-October. Powder the hedgehog with bug-killer to rid it of its parasites before you release it in your garden.

Hedgehogs usually have two litters a year, the gestation period is somewhere between thirty-one and forty days, and the lactation period about four weeks. The young are born blind, their eyes are open at fourteen days and, when three weeks old, they leave the nest, following mother in Indian file.

With luck your box will be occupied all the year, although hedgehogs won't necessarily raise families in it. During the spring and summer an individual may simply use it as a bedroom during the day. But of course he may well choose to hibernate in it when the time comes. Feed your hogs well in autumn, so that they face the long sleep with good reserves of fat. They may be fairly inactive in October if the weather is cold, but true hibernation starts much later and probably in December. Even after this the hedgehog may well make occasional sallies into the great outdoors. They usually emerge from hibernation in March.

You will soon get to know when the hedgehog comes out to feed and, if you provide a feeding station nearby, you will find that the animal is very tame and will take titbits, especially mealworms, from your hand. Avoid sudden noises, move and talk quietly.

One last warning. If you encourage hedgehogs, or any other animal for that matter, to live in your garden – do not use organochlorine garden pesticides of any kind.

Read: *Beneficial Insects*, by B. D. Moreton: Bulletin No 20 of the Min of Ag and Fish: published by HMSO.

Hedgehogs and the Gardener: published by the Henry Doubleday Research Association, Bocking, Braintree, Essex.

APPENDICES

A Organisations concerned with bird life

Royal Society for the Protection of Birds, The Lodge, Sandy, Bedfordshire SG19 2DL.

Illustrated journal *Birds*, free to members. Manages a network of bird reserves, organises many exhibitions and meetings, is much concerned with conservation and with the enforcement of the Protection of Birds Act. All birdwatchers should support this admirable and efficient society.

Young Ornithologists' Club, The Lodge, Sandy, Bedfordshire SG19 2DL. Associated with the RSPB, the YOC is the national club for young people (aged 7 to 15) who are interested in birds or want to learn about them. Quarterly magazine, *Bird Life*, nationwide projects, outings, courses. Kestrel badge.

The British Trust for Ornithology, Beech Grove, Tring, Hertfordshire HP23 5NR. Major link between amateur and professional ornithologists.

Minimum membership age, fifteen years. Members may take part in organised field studies, ringing and census work. Issues quarterly journal, *Bird Study*, six-weekly *BTO News*, invaluable field guides and other publications. Works closely with RSPB. Lending library. All serious birdwatchers should join. (Send for brochure.)

The British Ornithologists' Union, c/o The Bird Room, British Museum (Natural History), Cromwell Road, London SW7 5BD.

Senior bird society in Great Britain; its main object is the advancement of ornithological science on a world scale. Quarterly journal, *The Ibis*.

The Wildfowl Trust, Slimbridge, Gloucestershire GL2 7BT.

Illustrated annual report and periodical bulletins; maintains unique collection of swans, ducks and geese from all parts of the world.

Nature Conservancy Council (NCC), Northminster House, Northminster, Peterborough PE1 1UA.

County Naturalists Trusts and Bird Societies. Addresses are usually available at your local library.

The International Council for Bird Preservation (British Section), British Museum (Natural History), Cromwell Road, London SW7.
Issues annual report, co-ordinates and promotes international bird conservation.

The Henry Doubleday Research Association, 20 Convent Lane, Bocking, Braintree, Essex.
Issues newsletters and occasional publications of interest to the bird gardener. Initiates research into organic farming and gardening methods; pest control without poisons.

International Union for Conservation of Nature and Natural Resources, 1110 Morges, Switzerland.
Independent international body promoting and supporting action which will ensure the perpetuation of wild nature and renewable natural resources all over the world.

The World Wildlife Fund, 7–8 Plumtree Court, London EC4.
Raises funds and allocates them to projects covering a wide range from land purchase for national parks and reserves to ecological surveys and emergency programmes for the safeguarding of endangered plants and animals.

The Fauna and Flora Preservation Society, c/o The Zoological Society of London, Regent's Park, London NW1 4RY.

The Royal Society for the Prevention of Cruelty to Animals, Causeway, Horsham, Sussex RH12 1HG.

B Birds and the law

With certain exceptions, all wild birds, their nests and eggs, are protected, and the RSPB has prepared a useful summary of the law: The Wildlife and Countryside Act 1981 covers many subjects including the protection of animals, plants, habitats and national parks as well as the importation of endangered species. The main aspects concerning wild birds in England, Wales and Scotland which are included in Part 1 of the Act are given below.

DEFINITION OF A WILD BIRD
Any bird of a kind which is resident in or a visitor to Great Britain in a wild state. Game birds however are not included in the Wildlife and Countryside Act. They are covered by the Game Acts which fully protect them during the close season which is:
Pheasant, 2 February to 30 September
Partridge, 2 February to 31 August
Black Grouse, 11 December to 19 August
Red Grouse, 11 December to 11 August
Ptarmigan, in Scotland, 11 December to 11 August

BASIC PROTECTION
All birds, their nests and eggs are protected by law and it is thus an offence, with certain exceptions (see below) intentionally to:
1 kill, injure or take any wild bird,
2 take, damage or destroy the nest of any wild bird whilst it is in use or being built,
3 take or destroy the egg of any wild bird,
4 have in one's possession or control any wild bird (dead or alive) or any part of a wild bird which has been taken in contravention of the Act or the Protection of Birds Act 1954,
5 have in one's possession or control any egg or part of an egg which has been taken in contravention of the Act,
6 have in one's possession or control any live bird of prey of any species in the world (with the exception of Old World vultures) unless it is registered and ringed in accordance with the Secretary of State's regulations,
7 have in one's possession or control any bird of a species occurring on Schedule 4 of the Act unless registered (and in some cases ringed) in accordance with the Secretary of State's regulations

(NB for details of Schedule 4 species see Schedule 1),

8 disturb any wild bird listed on Schedule 1 while it is nest building, or at a nest containing eggs or young, or disturb the dependent young of such a bird.

SALE OF LIVE WILD BIRDS AND THEIR EGGS

Unless appropriately licensed it is an offence to sell, offer for sale, possess or transport for sale or exchange:

1 any live bird unless listed on Schedule 3, Part 1 and then only if aviary bred and close ringed with an approved ring as defined by the Secretary of State's regulations,

2 the egg of any wild bird (whether or not taken in contravention of the Act).

SALE OF DEAD WILD BIRDS

Unless appropriately licensed it is an offence to sell, offer, possess or transport for sale or hire any dead wild bird (or skin or part of such a bird) other than a bird on Schedule 3, Part II or III unless the vendor has been registered and the bird has been marked in accordance with regulations laid down by the Secretary of State.

Birds listed on Schedule 3, Part II may be sold dead at all times, those on Schedule 3, Part III may only be sold dead from 1 September until the 28 February.

Game birds may only be sold dead during the open season and for a period of up to 10 days immediately after the end of that season.

EXHIBITION OF WILD BIRDS

It is an offence to show at any competition, or in premises in which a competition is being held, any live wild bird unless listed on Schedule 3, Part I and ringed in accordance with the Secretary of State's regulations.

METHODS OF KILLING AND TAKING BIRDS

A number of methods of killing, injuring or taking birds are prohibited. These include gins, springs, traps (eg in the form of pole traps), snares, nets, bird lime, electrical scaring devices and poisonous or stupefying substances. The use of decoys of live birds tethered, blinded or maimed is also illegal.

BIRDS IN CAPTIVITY

In addition to the registration requirements for birds of prey and certain other Schedule 1 species (see Basic Protection: 6 and 7), it is illegal to keep any bird (excluding poultry) in a cage or other receptacle which is not of sufficient size to permit the bird to stretch its wings freely in all directions. Exceptions to this are if the bird is undergoing veterinary treatment, is in the course of conveyance or is being exhibited: in the latter case the time the bird is so confined should not exceed an aggregate of 72 hours.

ATTEMPTING TO COMMIT AN OFFENCE

It is an offence to attempt to commit any offence or have in one's possession anything capable of being used to commit an offence. The most notable exceptions to the above provisions are:

1 an authorised person (eg a landowner or occupier) may kill a bird listed on Schedule 2, Part II but not in Scotland on Sundays or Christmas Day; he may also destroy or take the nest or eggs of such a bird,

2 a person charged with killing or attempting to kill a wild bird other than one included on Schedule 1, shall not be guilty of an offence if he can show his action was necessary for the purpose of preserving public health or air safety, preventing spread of disease or preventing serious damage to livestock, foodstuffs for livestock, crops, vegetables, fruit, growing timber or fisheries, (see licences),

3 a person may take or kill (or injure in attempting to kill) a bird listed on Schedule 2, Part I outside the close season,

4 a person may *take* a wild bird if he can satisfy the court the bird had been injured other than by his own hand and that his sole purpose was to tend it and then release it when no longer disabled; or he may kill it if he can prove it was so seriously disabled as to be beyond recovery. Sick and injured birds listed on Schedule 4 should be registered with the Department of the Environment or passed to an approved keeper.

LICENCES

Licences may be issued by government departments to kill or take birds for the following purposes:

Scientific or educational
Ringing or marking
Conserving wild birds
Protecting any collection of wild birds
Falconry or aviculture
Taxidermy
Preserving public health or air safety
Preventing serious damage to livestock, foodstuffs for livestock, crops, vegetables, fruit, growing timber or fisheries
Killing a gannet for food on the island of Sula Sgeir
Taking a gull's egg for food
Taking a lapwing's egg for food before 15 April

Licences may also be granted for the sale of live birds (except those listed on Schedule 3, Part I) and the sale of dead birds or their parts; for scientific examination and photography of a Schedule 1 species at its nest and for the public exhibition or competition of birds not listed on Schedule 3, Part I.

FINES

The maximum fine that can be imposed in respect of a single bird, nest or egg receiving ordinary protection is £400. For offences involving a Schedule 1 species or an illegal method of killing (eg poisoning) the maximum is £2,000.

There are over 500 species of bird in Britain and as the Schedules only deal with a small number this sometimes confuses people. Please remember therefore that all birds, except those listed on Schedule 2 and Schedule 1, Part II are fully protected throughout the year.

SCHEDULE 1 — PART I

Birds protected by SPECIAL PENALTIES at all times

*Avocet
*Bee-eater
*Bittern
*Bittern, Little
*Bluethroat
 Brambling
*Bunting, Cirl
*Bunting, Lapland
*Bunting, Snow
*Buzzard, Honey
*Chough
*Corncrake
*Crake, Spotted
*Crossbills (all species)
*Curlew, Stone
*Divers (all species)
*Dotterel
*Duck, Long-tailed
*Eagle, Golden
*Eagle, White-tailed
*Falcon, Gyr
*Fieldfare
*Firecrest
 Garganey
*Godwit, Black-tailed
*Goshawk
*Grebe, Black-necked
*Grebe, Slavonian
*Greenshank
 Gull, Little
 Gull, Mediterranean
*Harrier (all species)
 Heron, Purple
*Hobby
*Hoopoe
*Kingfisher
*Kite, Red
*Merlin
*Oriole, Golden
*Osprey

 Owl, Barn
 Owl, Snowy
*Peregrine
*Petrel, Leach's
*Phalarope, Red-necked
*Plover, Kentish
*Plover, Little Ringed
*Quail, Common
*Redstart, Black
*Redwing
*Rosefinch, Scarlet
*Ruff
*Sandpiper, Green
*Sandpiper, Purple
*Sandpiper, Wood
 Scaup
*Scoter, Common
*Scoter, Velvet
*Serin
*Shorelark
*Shrike, Red-backed
*Spoonbill
*Stilt, Black-winged
*Stint, Temminck's
 Swan, Bewick's
 Swan, Whooper
*Tern, Black
*Tern, Little
*Tern, Roseate
*Tit, Bearded
*Tit, Crested
*Treecreeper, Short-toed
*Warbler, Cetti's
*Warbler, Dartford
*Warbler, Marsh
*Warbler, Savi's
*Whimbrel
*Woodlark
*Wryneck

Species marked with an asterisk must be registered (and in certain cases ringed) if kept in captivity. Registration also applies to ALL birds of prey in the world with the exception of Old World vultures.

SCHEDULE 1 – PART II
Birds protected by special penalties during the close season 1 February to 31 August\(21 February to 31 August below high water mark) but which may be killed or taken at other times.
Goldeneye
Greylag Goose (in Outer Hebrides, Caithness, Sutherland, and Wester Ross only)
Pintail

SCHEDULE 2 – PART I
Birds which may be killed or taken outside the close season 1 February to 31 August except where indicated otherwise.
Note: The close season for duck and geese when below high-water mark is 21 February to 31 August.
Capercaillie – close season 1 February to 30 September
Coot
Duck, Tufted
Gadwall
Goldeneye
Goose, Canada
Goose, Greylag
Goose, Pink-footed
Goose, White-fronted (in England & Wales only)
Mallard
Moorhen
Pintail
Plover, Golden
Pochard
Shoveler
Snipe, Common – close season 1 February to 11 August
Teal
Wigeon
Woodcock – close season 1 February to 30 September except in Scotland where 1 February to 31 August.

SCHEDULE 2 – PART II
Birds which may be killed or taken by authorised persons at all times.

Crow	Magpie
Dove, Collared	Pigeon, Feral
Gull, Great black-backed	Rook
Gull, Lesser black-backed	Sparrow, House
Gull, Herring	Starling
Jackdaw	Woodpigeon
Jay	

Birds which may be sold alive at all times if ringed and bred in captivity.

Blackbird	Linnet
Brambling	Magpie
Bullfinch	Owl, Barn
Bunting, Reed	Redpoll
Chaffinch	Siskin
Dunnock	Starling
Goldfinch	Thrush, Song
Greenfinch	Twite
Jackdaw	Yellowhammer
Jay	

SCHEDULE 3 — PART II
Birds which may be sold dead (at all times).
Pigeon, Feral
Woodpigeon

SCHEDULE 3 — PART III
Birds which may be sold dead from 1 September to 28 February.

Capercaillie	Pochard
Coot	Shoveler
Duck, Tufted	Snipe, Common
Mallard	Teal
Pintail	Wigeon
Plover, Golden	Woodcock

RSPB answers to common queries about bird Law

What birds are protected in Britain?
With a few exceptions, all birds, their nests and eggs are protected by law and anyone breaking this law is liable to a fine or imprisonment. The main exceptions are certain game birds and species classed as pests.

Is it against the law to collect birds' eggs?
Yes, with very few exceptions. The taking of just one egg of a common bird such as a blackbird or robin could result in a fine.

What about eggs from a deserted nest?
This is also illegal, for the reasons that it prevents someone taking eggs from a nest which he mistakenly believes is deserted, and prevents an unscrupulous person taking eggs from an occupied nest and saying that it had been deserted.

I have found a young boy collecting eggs, should I report him to the police?
No. It would be much better to explain to him why, as well as being illegal, egg collecting is rather pointless and selfish. Try to interest him in watching birds instead — tell him about our Young Ornithologists' Club and the many activities which the club

organises for young people.

Can I sell a collection of birds' eggs?

Only by obtaining a licence from the Home Office. Otherwise, the sale and exchange of birds' eggs is illegal.

What can I do about youths who shoot at birds with air guns in our local park?

Inform the police immediately. With few exceptions it is illegal to shoot at any birds and also the youths would be breaking the law by using an air gun in a public place.

A farmer near us is shooting hundreds of wood pigeons, rooks and crows on his land. How can I stop him?

You cannot. These birds are among the species classed as agricultural pests and the owner or occupier of the land is allowed to shoot them.

I would like to have a tame kestrel. Can I take a young one from its nest and rear it myself?

No. It is illegal and more important, unkind. It is also extremely difficult to rear a young bird – its parents can do a far better job.

Is it legal to photograph birds at the nest?

It is now illegal to disturb on or near a nest, by photography or otherwise, birds which are included in the First Schedule of the Protection of Birds Acts (about sixty of the more rare species) without a special licence from the Nature Conservancy Council. Although it is legal to photograph nesting birds of common species, even this should only be done by a really skilled photographer using the correct equipment – otherwise the birds may desert. Instead, try photographing birds at bird tables, bathing places, etc.

I want to ring birds. How do I start?

You may only ring birds if you have a licence issued by NERC. You may only use official numbered rings, which are issued by the British Trust for Ornithology, if you have a BTO permit; to obtain a BTO permit, you must have been fully trained by a BTO licensed ringer.

I want to put colour rings on some birds in my garden. Where can I buy these rings?

It is illegal even to colour-ring birds. Special licences are only granted to properly qualified ringers by NERC.

Is it legal to keep in captivity a sick or injured bird?

Yes, provided that you release it as soon as it is well and able to fend for itself The law also allows one to kill a bird which is so seriously injured, other than by one's own action, that it has no reasonable chance of recovery.

C   Treatment of sick, orphaned and injured birds

This is the advice given jointly by the RSPB and the RSPCA. Birds fall into human hands for a variety of reasons, of which accidents and mauling by cats are perhaps the most common. Whatever the cause, these birds are wild creatures and if you are prepared to care for them you must aim to return them to their own environment as soon as possible – in fact the law requires you to do so. A sick bird or an orphan should be handled as little as possible and should not be made into a pet. Some birds can become tame very easily and it will be difficult for them to be released; remember that only a completely healthy bird can survive in the wild. To care for any sick creature involves considerable time, money, and patience and if you are not prepared to take on this responsibility or if the bird is injured beyond recovery it is better to be realistic about this and have the bird humanely destroyed rather than allow it to suffer from neglect.

SUMMARY
1 Sick birds need quiet, warmth and darkness first.
2 Food should be given after an initial period of rest.
3 Diseases or injuries should be treated by a veterinary surgeon as soon as possible.
4 Birds beyond complete recovery should be destroyed humanely.
5 Do not attempt to clean oiled birds; contact the RSPCA.
6 Young birds should usually be left undisturbed.
7 Birds must be released as soon as possible.

CAPTURE AND HANDLING
It is usually difficult to catch an injured bird and careless handling may result in further injury. Most birds become quieter when in the dark and throwing a towel or blanket over a bird, and then transferring it to a suitably sized box, should be relatively simple. Handling must be firm but gentle, holding the wings close to the body to prevent injury. Many birds can give a nasty nip and an elastic band over the bills of crows and gulls will give some

protection; take care not to block the nostrils and be sure to remove it before release. Gloves should be worn when handling birds of prey and be especially wary of their talons. Extra care should be taken when dealing with large birds such as herons or gannets and no birds should be held near to anyone's face. Swans and geese use the wings for defence and great care should be taken when handling these species. Some diseases of birds are transmissible to man, but if you wash your hands after handling the bird the chances of your catching anything are very small. If you keep cage birds, never put the sick bird near them.

THE PATIENT
The common injuries of birds are fractures of bones in wings and legs, wounds of skin or muscle, loss of feathers and shock caused by accidents. A small superficial wound can be kept clean with mild antiseptic and water and will heal quickly. Shock is best treated by putting the bird in a well-ventilated, dark box in the warm and quiet for at least 1 hour. More serious wounds and fractures must be treated by a veterinary surgeon.

A bird that is not injured, but is ill, may have a number of diseases. If it is so ill that you are able to pick it up easily then it is probably beyond recovery. Diagnosis is difficult in birds but a veterinary surgeon may be able to advise and give appropriate treatment. The RSPB does not itself employ veterinary staff nor does it have the facilities to look after sick or injured birds.

HOUSING
The patient should be kept somewhere warm and should not be unnecessarily disturbed. The best accommodation for a small bird is a cage of the sort used by budgerigar and canary breeders, with a

wire front and solid roof, floor, sides and back. A standard budgerigar cage covered over, leaving the front partly uncovered, is adequate and a box with wire netting can also be made into something suitable. If the bird is very ill, the temperature should be raised to about 70°F (21°C), or up to 86°F (30°C) for smaller birds. If the bird is able to use a perch, then it will be happier if one is provided. Cover the floor with thick newspaper which should be changed daily. Food and water must be placed where it is easily available.

FOOD

The bird must eventually be fed (see also Orphan Birds) and the food you supply varies with the type of bird. Small birds can be divided roughly into seed and insect-eaters. Finches, buntings and sparrows are mainly seed-eaters, and they can be given a proprietary mixed bird seed. Robins, dunnocks, blackbirds, thrushes, and tits are chiefly insect-eaters, and some substitute for insects must be found. Pet shops sell a 'universal' food for insectivorous birds. A good substitute for this food is scrambled egg and a little moist crushed cereal. While you are organising seed or insect supplies, bread or cake crumbs will do as a makeshift, but *only* for the first day. Strips of lean meat are also good for insect-eating birds but these must be coated with a vitamin-mineral supplement. A bird, especially a young one, must never be fed for any length of time without such a supplement, as abnormalities of the bones will develop. A bird which has lost some blood may be given a little glucose solution to drink made up in the proportion of a tablespoon of glucose to a pint of water.

Larger birds, such as crows and gulls, will often eat any scraps, including soaked puppy biscuit and tinned dog or cat food. Gulls particularly enjoy strips of raw fish but, again, fish must not be fed for any length of time without a vitamin-mineral supplement.

Uneaten food must be removed to prevent spread of disease.

ORPHAN BIRDS

It is a common experience in spring and summer to find a young bird sitting on the ground or hopping about without any parent visible, and it is probable that the parents are away collecting food, or they may have been frightened by your approach and are waiting nearby. Fledglings (feathered young), especially owls, may leave the nest before they can fly and if you find one do not attempt to put it back in its nest, because you will disturb the other young birds. If the bird is in an exposed position put it in some cover, but not too far away, where the parents will find and feed it. If the young bird is unfeathered and has obviously fallen out of the nest by accident, it may be possible to find the nest and put it back. If, however, you are worried about a fledgling, go right away for two hours and return later to see if the bird still seems to be in trouble. If you must take the bird home then you should be prepared for a long, messy and time-consuming job, and you should not be too eager to take it on. You can never hope to give the bird the attention it would receive from its parents, and it will be difficult for it to learn to fend for itself properly in the wild.

Assuming that you have decided that there is no alternative to taking the bird home because it really has been abandoned, you must find suitable food for it. For regular feeding you can give crushed soaked biscuit mixed with a little scrambled egg and thin strips of ox heart or a few pieces of cut-up earthworm. Natural foods in the form of small insects such as greenfly, green caterpillars, ant cocoons, or cut up mealworm, can be given depending on the size of the bird. A vitamin supplement must always be added.

Use blunt forceps or tweezers for feeding if possible (a $\frac{3}{16}$in or $\frac{1}{4}$in paint brush could be used to feed small fledglings).

Moistening the food will provide all the water a young bird needs. If the bird is young enough you may find that touching its beak with the forceps is enough to make it gape and you can put the food well down its throat. If it does not gape, then you must gently prise the beak open with your thumb and forefinger and get someone else to push the food down. After two or three forced feeds the birds should learn to gape.

Young birds may eat their own weight of food during a day, and the young of small birds such as the robin should not go more than one hour without food, so feed your bird a quantity regularly every hour during daylight until it is feathered. Faecal sacs should be removed at each feed. Once it has been transferred to a cage, because it is too active to live in a box any longer, leave a pot of food and one of water in the cage to encourage the bird to feed itself. While it is unfeathered you can make the bird a 'nest' in a box with tissues, keeping the box covered between feeds. Keep the box out of draughts and remember that the mother would normally brood her young at night, so your orphan needs plenty of warmth. You can keep the box in an airing cupboard at night.

RELEASE

Birds must be released as soon as possible. Ideally they should be returned to the spot where they were found. If this is not possible, then there should be something at the release point which they can recognise and to which they can return. For a bird which has been kept indoors it is a good idea to take its cage or box to the release point and leave it there for an hour or so before you open it up. If possible, the release point should be where you can keep it under discreet observation, as the bird will tend to return to this place, usually at feeding or roosting times. It is also important to release birds early in the morning and preferably on a fine, warm day in order to give them time to settle down and feed, so that they do not go to roost with an empty crop. (Owls should be released at dusk.) Above all, make sure that the release point is in the type of place where the particular species of bird usually lives. You would not release a plover in woodland, for example, nor a woodpecker on Salisbury Plain!

It is unlikely that the bird will start fending for itself immediately and you may well have to put food out for it for several days, or until the food has remained untouched for three consecutive days. While the bird is still in captivity accustom it to regular feeding times, so that after release it will come back to the release point at those times and find food waiting. If you have had to keep the bird for more than a month it is going to need more time to adapt completely to the wild again. For this reason it is emphasised that birds should be released as soon as possible because prolonged captivity can cause additional hazards and stress.

SWANS AND OTHER WATERFOWL

Swans are often found tangled up in discarded fishing tackle and are also vulnerable to lead poisoning as a result of taking shot as grit. The RSPB is working to reduce these risks but it is not able to help in a practical way with injured or poisoned swans. The RSPCA will help in such cases.

BIRDS OF PREY

Birds of prey, which include owls, need raw meat, and although they rarely drink, a bowl of water is needed as they bathe a lot. When they start to recover, roughage such as rabbit's fur, hair or feathers should be added to their diet. Returning them to the wild is a difficult process and you should seek advice from a vet or the RSPCA.

STRANDED SEABIRDS

During strong gales, particularly westerlies, seabirds such as gannets, fulmars, and Manx shearwaters may get blown inland and find themselves stranded. These birds are usually tired and disoriented and can be fed with difficulty on strips of raw fish. They should be returned to the sea as soon as possible, releasing shearwaters in the evening or at night.

OILED BIRDS

If you find any oiled bird alive do not attempt to clean it yourself as it is a very specialised job and you may well do more harm than good. Carefully place the bird in a well-ventilated cardboard box, keep it warm and consult your local RSPCA inspector or a veterinary surgeon.

When large numbers of dead and live birds are coming ashore the RSPB should be informed as soon as possible (Sandy 80551).

POISONING

Gulls are often found in summer and autumn apparently paralysed and unable to lift their heads. This is likely to be the result of botulism poisoning, a naturally occurring toxin produced by bacteria. In this case and incidents involving *large* bird mortality the

RSPB should be informed of the location and number of birds involved.

HUMANE DESTRUCTION

It is natural to feel that a bird, however seriously injured, must be given a chance of life. A bird with a badly broken wing will seldom be able to fly again and a lame bird is severely handicapped in the struggle for existence.

In such cases it is better for the bird to be humanely destroyed and a veterinary surgeon will do this, but if you can bring yourself to undertake the job a heavy blow on the back of the head is quick and merciful.

INJURED WILD BIRDS AND THE LAW

It is not illegal to take in and keep most injured wild birds for the purpose of looking after them and eventually releasing them. Certain species, however, are required to be registered with the Department of the Environment before they can be legally kept, and these species are listed in Schedule 4 of the Wildlife and Countryside Act. This list includes *all* birds of prey (except owls) and most of Britain's rare breeding birds. The full list can be found in *Information about Birds and the Law* which is available from RSPB (please enclose two second class stamps).

If you find an injured Schedule 4 bird you should immediately contact a local RSPCA inspector or a vet who can legally hold it before transferring it to a Licensed Rehabilitation Keeper. Details of such keepers can be obtained from the Department of the Environment, Wildlife Licensing Section, Tollgate House, Houlton Street, Bristol BS2 9DJ.

More detailed information can be found in *First Aid and Care of Wild Birds*, edited by J. E. Cooper and J. T. Eley, published by David & Charles, 1979, and in *Care of the Wild* by W. J. Jordan and J. Hughes, published by Macdonald, 1982.

D   Bird topography

Putting a name to a bird is arguably the first requirement in getting to know something about it. And a knowledge of bird topography is an important foundation in the building up of identification expertise. Yet unfortunately the charts published in bird identification manuals offer such varied systems that they may confuse more than they help. The editors of *British Birds* magazine have produced these comprehensive and authoritative 'British Standard' charts in the hope that everyone will use the same language. The drawings are by Peter Grant.

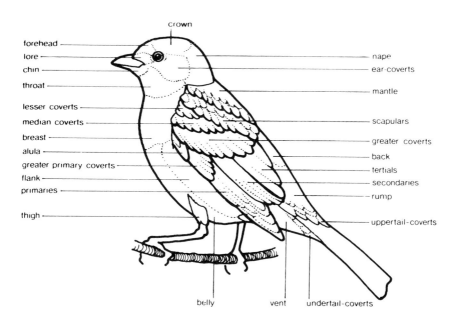

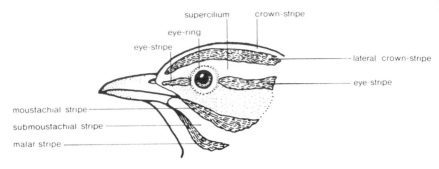

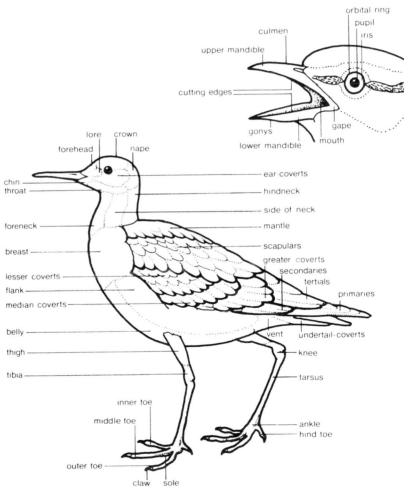

Standard bird topography charts reproduced by kind permission of Peter Grant and the editors of *British Birds* magazine

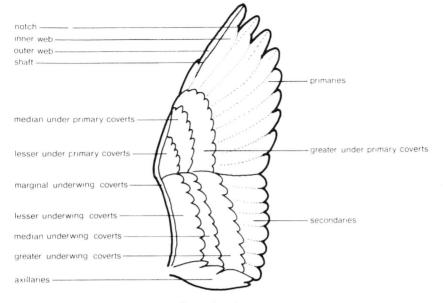

notch
inner web
outer web
shaft

primaries

median under primary coverts

lesser under primary coverts

greater under primary coverts

marginal underwing coverts

lesser underwing coverts

secondaries

median underwing coverts

greater underwing coverts

axillaries

Chart of underwing.

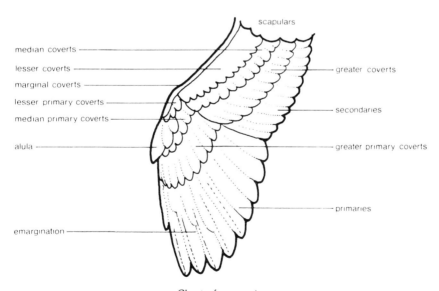

scapulars

median coverts

lesser coverts

greater coverts

marginal coverts

lesser primary coverts

secondaries

median primary coverts

alula

greater primary coverts

primaries

emargination

Chart of upperwing.

The 'tarsus' is actually the tarsometatarsus; the 'knee' is actually the intertarsal joint; the 'ankle' is actually the tarsometatarsophalangeal joint. We have, however, preferred the anatomically inaccurate but very much simpler and more easily understood terms

Further reading

Anon, *Nest Records Scheme*; BTO, Tring, Herts, 1972.

Atkinson-Willes, G. L., *Wildfowl in Great Britain*; HMSO, 1963.

Bannerman, D. A., *The Birds of the British Isles*; Oliver & Boyd, 1953–1963.

Batten, H. M., *How to Feed and Attract the Wild Birds*; Moray Press, 1933.

Boswall, J. H. R., *A Discography of Palaearctic Bird Sound Recordings*; Witherby, 1964.

Campbell, B., *Birdwatching for Beginners*; Penguin, 1952.

Campbell, B., *Finding Nests*; Collins, 1953.

Campbell, B., (ed), *A Dictionary of Birds*; T. & A. D. Poyser, 1985.

Chinery, M., *The Natural History of the Garden*; Collins, 1977.

Clegg, J., *The Observer's Book of Pond Life*; Warne, 1965.

Cramp, S., Simmons, K., *et al, Birds of the Western Palaearctic*; OUP, 1977.

Dennis, E., (ed), *Everyman's Nature Reserve*; David & Charles, 1972.

Drabble, P., *The Penguin Book of Pets*; Penguin, 1964.

Feu, Chris du, *Nestboxes*; BTO, Tring, Herts, 1985.

Fisher, J., (revised by Jim Flegg), *Watching Birds*; T. & A. D. Poyser, 1974.

Flegg, J., *Binoculars, Telescopes & Cameras for the Birdwatcher*; BTO, Tring, Herts, 1985.

Frazer, D., *Reptiles and Amphibians*; Collins, 1982.

Glue, D., *The Garden Bird Book*; Macmillan, 1982.

Hiesemann, M., (English edition), *How to Attract and Protect Wild Birds*; Witherby, 1908.

Hills, L. D., *Hedgehogs and the Gardener*; HDRA, 1965.

Hollom, P. A. D., (rev ed), *The Popular Handbook of British Birds*; Witherby, 1968.

Hudson, R., (ed), *A Species List of British and Irish Birds*; BTO, Tring, Herts, 1978.

Knight, M., *Bird Gardening*; Routledge & Kegan Paul, 1954.

Massingham, H. J., *Sanctuaries for Birds*; Bell, 1924.

Mead, C., *Robins*; Whittet, 1984.

Newton, I., *Finches*; Collins, 1972.

Nicholson, E. M., *Birds and Men*; Collins, 1951.

Perrins, C., *Birds*; Collins, 1976.

Perrins, C., *British Tits*; Collins, 1979.

Peterson, R. T., Mountfort, G. and Hollom, P. A. D. (rev ed), *A Field Guide to the Birds of Britain and Europe*; Collins, 1983.

Rudd, R. L., *Pesticides and the Living Landscape*; Univ of Wisconsin Press, 1965.

Simms, E., *British Thrushes*; Collins, 1978.

Smith, M., *British Amphibians and Reptiles*; Collins, 1951.

Soper, T., *Wildlife Begins at Home*; David & Charles, 1975.

Soper, T., *Everyday Birds*; David & Charles, 1976.

Soper, T., *Birdwatch*; Webb & Bower, 1983.

Southern, H. N., (ed), (rev ed), *The Handbook of British Mammals*; Blackwell, 1977.

Sparks, J. and Soper, T., *Owls*; David & Charles, 1971/1987.

Stebbings, R., *Bat Boxes*; FFPS, 1985.

Tottenham, K., *The Pan Book of Home Pets*; Pan, 1963.

Turner, E. L., *Every Garden a Bird Sanctuary*; Witherby, 1935.

Tweedie, M., *Pleasure from Insects*; David & Charles, 1968.

Vedel, H. and Lange, J., *Trees and Bushes*; Methuen, 1960.

Witherby, H. F. *et al*, (rev ed), *The Handbook of British Birds*; Witherby, 1952.

The Birdwatchers' Yearbook includes information on addresses and field work possibilities. Published by the Buckingham Press, Rostherne, Hall Close, Maids Moreton, Buckinghamshire MK18 1RH. *British Birds* magazine is published monthly. A bird-watchers' journal; not too scientific, not too 'pop'; includes monthly report on migrants and rarities. Free sample copy, plus subscription details, from Mrs Erika Sharrock, Fountains, Park Lane, Blunham, Bedford MK44 3NJ.

Acknowledgements

Spring 1965
My grateful thanks go to Mary Blair, Tom Edridge, Elaine and H. G. Hurrell, R. M. Lockley, Winwood Reade and E. H. Ware for ploughing through the first draft of this book and offering so much useful advice. David St John Thomas encouraged me to start; hundreds of BBC Spotlight viewers in the West Country forced me to continue (by asking questions, instead of answering them as I had requested). Chris Mead and David Wilson of the British Trust for Ornithology and Frank Hamilton and John Taunton of the Royal Society for the Protection of Birds have been most helpful. Many friends have encouraged me with good ideas and corrections; some have even valiantly improved my grammar, but the mistakes that remain are all my own work.

T.S.

Spring 1973
Since this book was first published, I have had a considerable correspondence with readers who have corrected and improved the information in it, and asked yet more questions. My sincere thanks to them; I think I have incorporated all the new material in this edition, but is is clear that no bird gardening book will ever be complete. So I throw in my hand again with a mixture of pleasure and trepidation.

T.S.

Spring 1977
At last . . . in colour! My thanks to all correspondents, even those who telephone in the middle of Dr Who. Also thanks to Robert Gillmor for his superb drawings and his enviable facility for doing them at the speed of flight, at least when pressure is firmly applied. And to Chris Mead and David Glue of the BTO, who combine scientific standards with an understanding of the enthusiasm of mere pleasure-bird-watchers. And to people like Mr and Mrs Pat Wilson who run the BTO's Garden Bird Feeding Survey, which collects and collates the hard facts. And to Pam Thomas of David & Charles, who makes publishing books fun. I tremble at the thought of what must surely come next – *The Bird Table Book in 3D*. Watch this space!

T.S.

Spring 1986

In its twenty-first year *The Bird Table Book* comes of age and reverts to its original title without the whizzkid appellations of 'new' or 'coloured' which decorated it in editions past. But never were truer words written than in my note of 1973 that 'no bird gardening book will ever be complete'.

My continuing gratitude to all those who have taken the trouble to write and to the stalwarts of the BTO who still enjoy birds more than they love their magic computer.

T.S.

Index

page numbers in italic indicate illustrations